Living On The Edge

BREAKING UP TO BREAK DOWN TO BREAKTHROUGH

Elizabeth Wilde McCormick

continuum
LONDON • NEW YORK

This book is dedicated to Ian Gordon Brown (1925–1996) with love and gratitude

Continuum

The Tower Building, 11 York Road, London SE1 7NX
370 Lexington Avenue, New York NY 10017-6503
www.continuumbooks.com

First published in this edition 2002

British Library Cataloguing-in-Publication Data
A catalogue record for this book is available from the British Library.

ISBN 0-8264-6780-6 (paperback)

Designed and typeset by YHT Ltd
Printed and bound in Great Britain by MPG Books Ltd, Bodmin, Cornwall

Contents

Introduction

This book attempts to explore the edges created by our everyday experience where inside and outside meet. In this place there is an opportunity to take a step beyond previous understandings. When what has drawn us in because of what is personal meets a transpersonal (that which goes beyond the personal) potential, we have the possibility of awakening to the kind of spaciousness in which there is more room to live and be. This may be finding a sense of meaning for what is happening to us. It may also amount to awakening to a spiritual understanding and the beginning of spiritual practice. The edge then becomes the bridge into wider experience. It also becomes the place where hardened edges are dissolved because we are less polarized or split and able to become aware of the whole, of the interrelationship between all living things. We can then build on finding a way of being that makes this space more available to ourselves individually and to others caught up in defending edges that only cause division and fear.

The book offers maps and understandings that help in naming edges and our fears of them. This approach to witnessing and naming may help us to become edge walkers – able to walk the edge and be there for others as they come after us.

The text is supported by the use of images that are often used to name the experience of being on the edge: the cliff; the ocean; the desert; the trap; the sword; the cave; the tightrope; the volcano.

Each has a landscape of feeling and quality. Each has aspects which are explored in Part Two. Each image and aspect has potential dangers and limitations as well as opening to that step into something new and wider. Most of us will be able to relate to each of the images at some point in our life.

PERSONAL EDGES

So what does it mean, to live on the edge?

We may all recognize the expression and be able to relate to the pull of the edge. But what *is* our personal edge? How do we get invited into it, and how can we transform our experience of the edge so that it expands rather than freezes us upon it?

All of us can trace periods of time when we felt pushed to the edge of our personal capacity for coping. We wonder how we can go on; we wonder how we can bear it a minute longer. This may be connected to life crises, to others' demands of us, to those things we thought we knew and understood but find we no longer do, to our capacity for tolerance, to being over-whelmed by difficult feelings, or to a deeper struggle with the root metaphor for our life, with connecting to why we continue to live, and on what terms we should live.

Most of us today are familiar with the edges between being and doing; between the 'me' who is seen by others and the outside world, and the private, perhaps hidden, 'me'.

We may reach edges where it is we who draw the line saying 'beyond this I will not go' and this may be to do with finding our individual or collective principles, or connecting with systems of morality or meaning.

We may feel at times that we need an edge in order to have something to go on because it is at the edge that we feel most intensely. Edges force decisions; what or who goes where. It is at the very edges of personal experience that a human being is most stretched and tested. At the edge, we meet our demons and our gods. We meet our potential for feeling alive and 'real'.

DANGER AND OPPORTUNITY

Sometimes we are stretched creatively by having an edge. The structure of the edge, its deadline effect, brings out our very best.

Sometimes we shrink from the edge and can only hover precipitously, feeling 'on hold', in limbo, paralyzed by fear for what the edge might bring. Sometimes we plunge over the edge into our personal darkness.

Bearing the tension of the place of the edge can also bear fruit, or call forth an awakening. A small beak of infant chick gestated inside an egg breaks through the edge of shell to signal new life. Green shoots of spring press through the frosted earth edge of winter. These moments of realizing and transcending the edge are always compelling. They are both thrilling and potentially dangerous. They offer, as do all edges which lean into crises, danger and opportunity.

Outside edges push us against the boundaries of ourselves and our everyday consciousness. To grow wise we have to find ways of meeting many edges.

We may court the edge; we may become addicted to the edge; we may get pushed onto the edge by outside circumstances.

As I write this new edition of *Living on the Edge* – first published in 1997 – the images of 11 September are still overwhelming and will become imprinted on my consciousness. The tension of opposite forces and ideas since this date asks us to be alive to many difficult and new edges. What is our attitude to power – political, religious, and economic? And how are we with the attitudes of others when they conflict with our own? Collectively, we are, in the year 2002, linked to the edge of two centuries. The current powerful forces are connected to power, religious belief and energy and the earth.

These systems, from time immemorial a central part in the life of human beings, have been pushed to the edge and the question is what will break under the pressure and what will transform and be redeemed. Our world in some areas now groans under the weight of overpopulation, and labours against global pollution and plunder. The progress myth of urban expansion and technological advance threatens and challenges the meaning and dignity of human expression. Any sentient person questions the nature of survival into the next century. What will be the values of the next millennium? On what terms will we live? We wonder, can we go back and harness the ancient wisdoms of the past in order to find ways to live that do not threaten the actual

3

fabric of the earth upon which we depend? Or, have we gone too far, become so dependent upon technological communications that our human muscles have grown slack?

Or, can we harness both developments in our life as human beings so that we come to the narrow path of the edge with wider, deeper funds of knowledge, from both East and West? From both artist and scientist? From both masculine and feminine principles? But use it for a shared purpose.

BECOME AN EDGE WALKER

Knowing what our personal edges are and what forces lead us there can be a way of becoming an edge walker. We know then that there will be edges. And that they teach us how to live even in the narrowest of places. Once we have recognized, walked, danced even, upon the many edges that invite us, we forge within ourselves a strong centre. This centre connects us with the ability to live in everyday terms and at the same time not to be limited by these terms. We do not become seduced by, held captive, thrown over, collapsed into the edge any more than our journey demands. An opportunity to widen our understanding can emerge from our dance upon the edge that cannot be realized in any other way. From the narrow place a breadth of strength and wisdom is forged.

From the edge we get to know our extremes. The opposite forces within us have the opportunity both to keep their vital differences and to come together via the edge in a way that offers the true heartfelt energy of transformation. Then the edge becomes the place where we are invited to view most carefully the divisions that divide us, both internally and externally and in our relationship with others and the world.

CONTROL OR CONTEMPLATION

Many people hunger for connection and relationship that is nourishing and which lasts. Searching for this externally may be exciting and is part of the offerings of our outside world, but this can never meet the deeper levels of our being where we long for that close association best described as the mindful love of our deepest heart. Those who seem to carry this essence are often the people who have nourished their spiritual practice and returned to the everyday with a deep sense of calm and love that glows from the inside and offers a light to us to be guided by. Many people are recognizing a need for contemplative and spiritual life that provides sustaining nourishment.

An experience at the edge – however this edge may present itself, and there are myriad of forms – can be the edge that awakens us to a more spiritual dimension. We may not be able to name it as such at the time and our experience may not be recognized by others.

SOUL MAKING AND SPIRIT RISING

This book describes how our personal edges can be places where we forge a deeper connection with our personal experience in terms of the hand we are dealt in this life. Soul making refers to the process of deepening event into experience. When we learn to embrace our life experience, we become more connected to the possibility of meaning within it and this process in itself lightens our load. When we are not victims of any system of understanding, we have a lighter heart with which to come to all experience and to see it just as it is. From this lighter place of connection with what is personal we are able to step nearer to experiences which are transpersonal.

By being awake to the transpersonal and soul dimensions, we become connected to all animate life, and are able to listen and respond to this note as its rhythm resonates throughout all the living and created world. In this way, our world becomes a wider vision of all that we create both individually and as a collective force. We are not reduced, as psychology would often reduce us, to a limited world of inner pathology mirrored in outside event. By being prepared to embrace soul making we may experience the rising of our spirit where we are lifted up above the smallness of need and desire into realms of wider love. This experience means we have to be prepared to meet the depths of our personal experience. Soul and spirit then become a twofold path. Going 'down' and going 'up' are part of the same journey. We cannot tread a spiritual path without being prepared to enter into the soulful depth experience of being human in all its ways. An image that well describes this is in Dante's *Divine Comedy* where his journey must take him down into what has been personal, before he can rise with Beatrice and enter paradise. Dante first tries to scale the mountain as if by will, but is sent back by three beasts, lion, leopard and wolf which represented for him pleasure, pride and greed, which he faced during his journey of descent into the realms of hell. In Buddhist philosophy, the three poisons are seen as craving, aversion (rage, negativity) and ignorance (denial).

THE ROOTS OF THIS BOOK

The understanding within this book comes from my work as a psychotherapist with a wide background in clinical work, in social psychiatry, cognitive analytic therapy, humanistic and transpersonal psychology. And from my meditative and mind-fulness practices based upon the work of Thich Nhat Hanh. And from my own experience as a human being on the edge.

The main psychological and philosophical themes come from my involvement with transpersonal psychology for the last twenty-two years. The use of the image of the spiral comes from recent understanding that the spiral shape is at the core of our microscopic cell and plant structures, all life grows from this shape. And in the journey of a human life, we tend to move in the way of the spiral, with life itself taking us back over the same place but from a different perspective.

Living on the Edge seems to have emerged quite naturally as a progression from my interest in and studies of the heart and of breakdown that have been the subject of my earlier books from 1984 onwards. In *Breakdown* I describe 'on the edge' as the second phase of the breakdown curve. Since *Breakdown* was first published in 1988, I see more and more people who use this expression spontaneously and who are negotiating edges of many different elements.

As a personal theme, I have always been aware of living close to the edge and sometimes my life has rendered this edge pretty thin. In May 1992 I had the following dream.

> I am running along the cliff edge in Suffolk where I live, with the North Sea on my left. I am in a hurry. Something taps at my right shoulder. I brush it off impatiently, rushing on. It taps again, and again I brush it off. At the third tap, however, I turn round impatiently. A young man, dressed casually, with a patient, kind face is standing behind me. He is pushing a young woman who slumps pale and lifeless in a wheelchair. 'All we want' he says, 'is permission to put up her easel'.

This dream speaks to many themes. To 'hurry sickness'; to being split between an overvalued, rational masculine and an under-valued, malnourished feminine; and to the sinister aspect of going too fast along a cliff edge. At the time, I knew that it was a vital dream, full of significance. I knew, in my head, that I had not given enough time to the 'artist' within, and I felt sickened, and terrified about this. But at the time I was unable to be fully awake to this reality and understanding by analysis is limited. My addiction to the illusion of hurry sickness as control meant that I was unable to enter into meditative practice fully, making the surrender needed, until through physical illness I was forced to stop and enter the dark. The potency of the dream was only fully revealed to me when I had actually to live body and soul, 'on the edge'. In June 1992, one month after the dream, I became seriously ill with viral meningitis, encephalitis and labyrinthitis which took me to and beyond the edge for the next two and a half years.

I honour this experience because it so beautifully illustrates Jung's understanding that we can 'know' something in the head, even write about it, but it is only when it touches us in the heart that we *truly* take note of it. I could make sense of my dream and work with the images, but when *they* really got hold of me their intent was awe-inspiring. Awe-inspiring because it is so often just when we think we have sorted something out that we are most challenged. It reminds us that some much greater force is alive and well inside us that is not connected to the control of the ego and whose path we are humbled to follow. It means that we must *never* reduce the power of the dream or waking image to rationality or intellectual presumption, but let *it* tell us. And how it does!

There is a large collective myth that if we can maintain control we will be fine. This is reflected in our politics, the way countries use arms and force to get their way, to defend themselves. But what this does is to make the unheard and unvalued more marginalized and eventually more militant. Then violence and force become the only communication. Images of twin towers prevail.

There is an omnipotent myth within psychotherapy and analysis that if you have worked hard on yourself and done enough therapy you are 'sorted', even 'whole'. And the fantasy is that this means never becoming unwell or getting out of balance.

A few people were cross with me for becoming so seriously ill, prey to judgements that I had not worked hard enough on my internal conflicts. But many people offered me their unconditional friendliness, their loving kindness and acceptance. It was as if they trusted me to go through this difficult process and come through. My gratitude for this is still fresh. I believe that my eventual emergence from this place depended in part upon the attitude of others. Their wise midwifery was to stand alongside me and name the process of initiation, when I could not see it. They watched me struggle with myself before making suggestions, and held my hand in the darkest terrors when I was haunted by the thought of damage to my brain.

Since this time I have faced another edge and trodden the well-worn path following bereavement after the death of my husband John who died in May 1999. Being privileged to be present at the moment of his death as his spirit left his body has allowed me to move along another edge, that of life and death, and to find that line so much less defined and absolute than I had imagined. To witness his departure was to be convinced about the difference between spirit and body and that our bodies and personalities are only one of the vehicles we inhabit during this lifetime. What helps us to live, tolerate and love our life are the communications we must endeavour to have between inhabiting spirit and incarnate demand.

The process of grief pulls us into many edges of emotional

pain. The oceanic swirl of feelings, a chasm or pit opening up in the absence of the loved one, dark rages of the unfairness of being left alone when the world appears to be in pairs. Walking this edge became possible because I had some learning of the language of emotion and found places to be present with the huge mix of feeling and no feeling. Again, I was supported by kind hands. And, at this more recent experience of the edge, I was in daily mindfulness practice which allowed me to have a place within myself that was actually not suffering. That was beyond pain and all its attachments of mind. I also began to understand that value of daily reminders of the nature of impermanence, that everything is changing all of the time. The illusion we try to hold onto is one of permancence. Death challenges us to find ways to sit with itself as the only certainty there is.

My view has always been that wholeness must include health and sickness, light and darkness, and the potential for good and evil. This book does not offer a solution but a journey of exploration. In risking and embracing the liminal space, which I call the edge, we become edge walkers; we learn to survive in the narrowest of places; we may find that the edge as a liminal space offers us an experience of non-attachment that strengthens our commitment to spiritual practice. We may find that in embracing the many facets of the edge we are ready to serve others who must find their way.

Part One

MAPPING THE EDGE

1

General Images and Definitions of the Edge

The edge is often defined and experienced as a narrow place, limited and defined by the purpose it serves, to make distinction between the hinterlands on either side. It is also a liminal place where paradox and ambiguity reign. It is like one description of the state of an embryo where energies that are 'neither living nor dead from one aspect, and neither living and dead from another' are in process. This ambiguity and paradox is our challenge – to not get caught into the splitting or polarization the edge can create which results in stalemate, nor to become overwhelmed by the confusion of the liminal and its 'no place'.

An edge tends to be formed by two or more things. We have darkness and we have light and the space in between forms an edge. We have the fast descending nightfall in Africa and the liminal space of dusk or dawn, of Europe. This can be seen as the place where one aspect is in retreat and the other in advance.

THE EDGE AS BOUNDARY

Edges serve as boundaries between one place or state of being and another. We can see this in terms of the emotional forces inside us, when we come up against an edge such as anger, fear or loss. We can also see the edge as being outside of ourselves, connected to other people, accommodation, jobs, food.

Even though narrow by definition, the edge may spread out to form a border, margin or verge, we may experience it as a cave, cliff, cage or desert, and it may carry the energy of a volcano or sword or tidal wave.

When the edge serves as a boundary it may be clear and robust, marked by potted plants, the songs of birds or by army personnel with guns. Or, as in 'verge' it may describe a slow meandering into something as in 'verging on', meaning, nearly or almost; we say 'verging on a nervous breakdown'.

The edge can be formed by a brim or rim. When liquid reaches the limits of its container it is at the brim, it can also brim over; and we can brim over with affection or with fury, on the edge of sensing that our feelings are running over the brim or boundary, and into the next space. 'My cup runneth over'.

Margins of a page separate text from binding and give space for notes and anecdotes. People get shoved into the margins of society when they are poor or homeless and become margin-alized.

We speak of brinkmanship, taking a challenge to its utmost tension, the edge of surprise.

Too tight a boundary and we keep too much out and what is inside suffers and festers for lack of change. Too loose a boundary and all energy is scattered and the centre cannot hold.

THE EDGE AS DEFENCE

When we want to keep others out, we build a wall inside us, or our body language shuts them out. We may need, and choose, to do this and it may serve us well. But defences are never permanent. They may be built like external structures, with great effort and imagination, designed to withstand pressure and encroachment and they may last for years until challenged by greater forces. Like the sea defences in Suffolk and the great barbed and armoured wall that divided Berlin. It is as if defensive edges are built to be challenged, and changed, even edges that seemed so permanent. And behind the falling of each of the well-documented great structures is the huge, often unconscious collective pressure for change, whether from Nature's elements or from cultural pressure. So that when the edge is breached and changed we must all change. And when we hold onto our internally built defences for too long we remain inaccessible, we lose the ability to communicate, our inner world becomes cut off, at risk of an autistic silence.

THE EDGE AS SOMETHING SHARP

The edge can also be something sharp, the thin blade of a sword, a knife edge. There are emotional edges to strong feeling, to anger, rage and to violence, and the edges of despair and misery may offer a boundary on intensity beyond which our feelings sharpen and harden. We may be emotionally sharpened by edginess in the atmosphere, sharpened by the drama of violence and hatred, on the streets of Lebanon, or a performance of *Macbeth*. These things pierce into us with their edge. Voices get an edge when under threat or siege. Edges of fear and terror press into us with cold steel. There are sharp edges in nervous excitement, irritation and expectation. We feel the edge of our fury, our own potential for thrusting with the sword of violence and it is all we can do to keep our hand in our pocket.

Our edges get sharpened when we want an advantage, when we are at the 'cutting edge' of science or new ideas.

DYNAMIC AND RIGID EDGES

Edges keep things out and they also keep things in. When the edge becomes rigid it may not be able to let anything pass. It may just become a grotesque white elephant, crumbling slowly with time like the stone walls and barricade that once formed the penal colony of Port Arthur in Tasmania, where children had cells and penal servitude for life was the norm. They remain as stubborn ruins, to remind us of the rigid structures we once created to try to maintain one fixed view of human behaviour.

And we fill our land with the waste products of consumerism, plastic, bottles, cans, nappies, whose dead structures with their lethal edges no longer serve but threaten.

When edges are dynamic, they are in movement and thus are open to change. Like an elastic band or flexible friend this edge may move with us at our own pace. As we change, so the edge changes. We bounce ideas, form thoughts, take on the edges of others, expand our awareness.

Even within the body itself, we can witness the rigid edges of 'disease' which has formed a structure needing to be reduced by chemotherapy, cut by scalpel, replaced by transplant, endured as an arthritic limb in a wheelchair, and also those structures which seem to have dynamic form and are therefore temporary. For example, dynamic constrictions of the coronary arteries, caused by the mind's response to stress, are changed by rest. Palpitation and stomach cramp, which can create the sharpness of spasm or the rigid outline of ulceration may be created by panic attack due to unprocessed feeling, and might soften and heal in response to a listening ear rather than action upon the structure. Sometimes the edges need both responses.

NATURAL AND UNNATURAL EDGES

Some edges are natural, formed by the geography of outside such as the edge that comes between two mountains to form a valley or pass. The beach or cliff are the interface between land and sea. And these outside images are often taken inside symbolically. Walking in the valley of the shadow of death; the cliffhanger in decision making and games of dice or cards, even now in medical diagnoses, and cliffs, as at Beachy Head, can offer the literal places for the edges of life and death.

Each structure we create as humans produces an edge between the natural outside geography and the object created. We could say then that these edges are unnatural because they belong to the world of humans and are forced upon our natural habitat. Some structures such as harbours and houses may be built in sympathy with the land and seem to flow naturally out of it. We glory then in the meeting between man/woman-made creative object and the natural poetry of the landscape. Others, such as electric pylons and high-rise hotels, can appear like unnatural intrusions, their alien edges as blots on the landscape.

Cramped rooms may make us feel the edges pressing in on us; or, we may have to fortify the edges of our space with barriers, locks and wire. In simple terms, tables and chairs give form and edge to delineate where we sit and eat or make our bed. Fences may provide an edge for roses, clematis, for the perch of robin and finch.

These edges are in relationship to what we make of them internally, our perception of the moment influences how they are seen. Often the outside structures we create mirror the world we carry inside us. Perhaps there are times when we can only see ourselves as cramped and overcrowded inside, or when we feel homeless as if we have no root, and at other times we are able to use more space, stretch out into new rooms and passages. When boundaries are not created we can feel overwhelmed or lost, looking for something to define us or give us shape.

LANGUAGE

Language has always carried a certain edge. It keeps us out if we have not learned it. Many different languages are now available for us to learn. Growing media coverage from different parts of the globe means that we are aware of the range of different languages, and the lack of communication if we cannot share them. Alongside a collective need for communication, individual languages are being lost – over two thousand languages have been lost from the Pacific Islands. Some countries such as Wales and Ireland work hard to keep their language inheritance as their unique badge of identity.

Nor does language define us as clearly in the context of education, social class or economic group, which can be helpful, enabling, growing. But there are also losses, of style and music in language, often replaced by a bland character-free note, or a string of jarring expletives.

EDGES SHAPED BY SOCIETY, CULTURE, TECHNOLOGY AND RELIGION

In western society and culture, there are fewer clearly defined social and moral edges. Those edges, once held by family, state or religion, are held by the individual. Women who give birth out of wedlock are no longer considered morally defective as in the 1920s and placed in institutions or sent to the workhouse. Fewer women are forced into aborting or giving their child away for adoption, and, those who do, do so from a place of choice. Children born to parents who are either not legally married, or multiply married, are increasing in numbers. Thus the boundaries of the family, once tightly controlled by church law and society, become an ever-expanding changing unit of steps, fosters, boy and girlfriends.

Stories of personal tragedies, once a private matter for personal conscience and the balm of confession, are now sold shamelessly to newspapers for vast sums of money. The surge of litigation against professionals or personal friends to relieve revenge or simply as a response to mistake, misunderstanding or once accepted sad happenings seems epidemic. Professions are also specializing as a result, developing 'experts'. Soon therapists will also be divided into specialities and will be unable to give their common-sense opinion if they are not 'accredited' as to the speciality upon which they comment. The reluctance or lack of courage to accept personal responsibility when appropriate has moved us as a society into the realm of magic control with no effort where it is always someone else's fault. The state or the law then has to become arbiter to try to solve what were once personal disputes, polarizing opinion and the fortunes of many. We ask them to be the edge for us, relieving us of the very necessary limits that the edge provides.

If there is no societal boundary on shameful exploit we never face our own shame and work through its reality, so its hold on us is less unconscious and liable to projection. It feels hard for common sense to survive among the relegation of these edges away from the personal. These edges of morality once held the boundary for how to behave, they gave us something to go on so that we knew where we were. Then, having the edge clearly defined, we could push against it or abandon it and take the consequences, or we could allow the edge to shape our personal life.

It is possible to 'sin' in the old-fashioned sense, and get away with it externally in society's terms. Stealing money, cheating on a business partner, drunk driving, murder, adultery, no longer necessarily lead to loss of friendship or transportation, let alone being beheaded for treason! Countries where the boundaries of the law for crime are fierce but clear, such as having your hand cut off, are penalized by more liberal countries whose crime rate soars. Sin as defined by excommunication from a system of meaning, confined to hell for eternity, is less of a fear except where Catholicism and Islam prevail as religious structures which hold the social system in their web.

The advance of technology has brought many new edges. There are more objects to understand and look after. There are greater edges between those who have material goods and the benefit of money and education and those who do not. In western industrialized nations there are more decisions to make over how we should treat our bodies, such as accepting an organ transplant or foetal implant; taking powerful medications that alter mood and behaviour. Just a few thousand miles away the majority of people hunt daily for their 800 calories needed for survival, or die of starvation. The life expectancy in Nepal is 45 years.

So often in our western culture it is the ego functions of control, extroversion and performance that become valued and admired, with any fragility, uncertainty and woundedness rejected and repressed, or marginalized by harsh judgement. It is hard for a soulful dimension to be recognized when ego control has rigid edges. There are vivid global imaages. The hard-edged bullets developed by sophisticated technology are splattered into the impoverishment of African countries, feeding the addiction to power for its own sake, for ego gratification. Addiction to possessions, fashion, money for money's sake, gets in the way of the wisest use of natural resources, the earth's minerals, the oceans, the atmosphere in the sky above us involving the air we breathe. A high-rise hotel with gold-fitted bath taps rises out of a desert culture or a large city where women, children and young people beg in the streets and waste pollutes the rivers. These extremes exist. We also have the means to address them. At a European Conference on transpersonal psychology, the psychologist James Fadiman spoke of two practical acts each individual could offer as part of their enlightened living. Plant a tree and bury a gun.

Many of the moral and spiritual decisions we must make about prolonging life emerge on the edge of these advancements. They are edges that require our wisdom.

PEOPLE LIVING AT THE EDGE

There are few human groups who have not built structures. Until colonization by white westerners, the Aboriginal people lived all over the vast continent of Australia building nothing and creating no pollution. They are thought to be over 50,000 years old, the oldest living group of people in our history. In their nomadic tradition they use a piece of land until it is in need of rest and replenishment, then they move on to let the land regenerate for other groups or for their return wanderings. Their edges and boundaries are interconnected like a honeycomb of spiritual, physical and cultural sharing, the needs of the group to eat, sleep, protect themselves from the elements, and to sing, dance and create ritual for change.

Traditional travelling, Gypsy, tribal and nomadic people have always been linked closely with the earth and the natural world as well as being seen to carry special psychic and prophetic gifts. They know the rhythms of the seasons and the movements of the stars and planets. They live simply. They may be carrying much of the soul and spirit of the world today. This is their only home. Often judged as 'antisocial', they in fact feel that 'to behave antisocially is the proper expression for their marginal condition'.[1] For Travelling people there is nothing more spiritual than the natural world itself, putting oneself above it

---

[1] Wilde, K. "Comparisons with hunter-gatherer societies of the American continent – environmental ethic and the shamanic roles". BA Dissertation (1990).

would be pointless and dangerous. It provides everything needed for life. It is life.

People become marginalized when they cannot or do not find ways of fitting into social norms. At all edges of society and culture lie the shanty towns, encampments, temporary accommodation for people on the edge of the main social group. Tramps, bag ladies, vagabonds, beggars and squatters are part of all major cities and sophisticated cultures. They forge their own places out of what has been discarded; they recreate 'home'.

EXPLORERS

There are many who court the edge and those prepared to put themselves on the edge in order to bring back news of events in other countries. Men and women who go over the borders to record the new and evolutionary edges of other countries and cultures, the war correspondents and photographers, whose home is a tent and mouthpiece their lens or letter. Then there are menders and healers, those professionals working within Médecins sans Frontières.

The explorers of mountains, oceans depths, ice caps, put themselves on the edge of both the outside geography and their inside selves, sometimes 'touching the void' like Joe Simpson in the Andes. Firefighters, potholers, all rescuers, work on the edge to meet others who have fallen from or lie clinging to the edge.

THE ARTIST'S EDGE

Artists perhaps offer us a unique glimpse of the edge walker and they often have periods in and out of internal edges such as 'madness' or delusion and depression. In common with travelling or nomadic people, artists need to be able to put themselves on edge in order to create in the faithful image of their ideal. Turner once had himself roped to the mast of a ship in full storm in order to capture the visual image of the light; the movement and feeling of the water. In the *Artist's Eye*, Harriet Shorr writes: 'The gesture of the brush is an expression of feeling

21

aroused by the perception. Painting is not about objects themselves but about the process of seeing and painting them'. Artists often need to live in seclusion or as recluse, maintaining a position as outsider, and actually live on the edge of the group or society in order to be the observers, recorders and commentators of the group and its history as a whole. Within their work, each working day involves artists pushing themselves against the boundaries of what has gone before in order to create the new. Thus we have the 'cutting edge'; 'concert pitch'.

The artist within

We all have an inner artist who paints the inner life onto the canvas interface between inner and outer. Thus the creation of everything in which we become fascinated and involved. Our dreams and fantasies, our hopes and fears, the way we play, those images and people and experience we are drawn towards are all initiated by the inner artist. The colours and shapes we choose, sound and dance with which we move, the tapestries we weave throughout our life all originate via the inner artistry of each individual.

When we look back and see the themes and threads of our life so far, we can see the hand of the artist who has woven his or her way, always holding some thread or other, linking the different phases of our life. Even our symptoms, whether through body, mind or emotions, are created by the artist who uses whatever tools are available to make sure this language is kept alive. Symptoms are our main signalling device from our unconscious world. Much of this book will be drawing upon the inner artist to help us become edge walkers.

PSYCHOLOGICAL EDGES

Most of us tend to experience ourselves in parts. Part of us may feel small and helpless, like a child, while another is fierce and grown up. One part may feel angry but is hidden by a need to smile and please. Usually, we grow as a person in fits and starts, a 'survival self' growing larger than other more undeveloped parts. Sometimes we feel that part of us is blocked. Because we can be flexible and self-reflective, the divisions between these parts of ourselves have dynamic edges, and can be changed.

We all need appropriate boundaries as we filter information, deal with crises. Systems get blown when the edges get overloaded, as in some experiences of rage or grief. Or when the unconscious life of a person fills all available space, the boundaries holding the personality together breakdown, and the centre cannot hold, as in some forms of breakdown.

Problems seem to occur when edges between one inner state of being are too rigid and the parts have become split off, separated from awareness of the living whole, as in dissociation, or multiple personality states. Too poorly defined edges between consciousness and unconsciousness can result in psychosis and schizophrenia.

The divisions between knowing and not knowing, feeling and not feeling, between what constitutes madness and sanity are all open to question and opinion. But we long for an edge to define for us; to give us clear guidelines, a clear path to follow, to gain us some control. The liminal periods in between our stages of life and development are periods where nothing is certain, where the nature of our footsteps creates the path itself. In this in-between place, we are most likely to be open enough to nurture a spiritual dimension.

HEALTH AND SICKNESS

All people in mental institutions and psychiatric hospitals are on the edge. They are travelling in the borderlands between what we term 'madness' and 'sanity'. Their lives, for a time, are in the hands of professionals whose belief systems about their predicament will rule treatment. The edges between madness and reason have, throughout history, been hotly debated. In *Psychiatry Inside Out: Selected Writings*, Franco Basaglia writes:

> Over the centuries, the rational and the irrational come to coexist, while remaining separate. Yet they are drawn closer once reason is in a pos-

ition to neutralise madness by recognising it as part of itself, as well as by defining a separate space for its existence. Such a process does not merely represent the evolution of science and knowledge. Nor does it signify the transition of madness from tragic experience in the world to sin, guilt, scandal, condemnation, and objectification of unreason – elements which, in our critical view are still fused and present in madness.

Anyone who exhibits wild, highly emotional or altered states, who sees visions, hears voices, dresses in a non-conformist mode challenges the social civilized order. Without a spiritual perspective, this will become the boundary. The information from those who have gone beyond the frontiers will be lost, the voices go unheard and the visions unshared, the images uncharted. Those who have spent time in mental asylums and written about their experiences: John Perceval, novelist Antonia White, William Styron, Anne Sexton, are all able to impart, with poetic clarity and reason, the stark images of their suffering while 'mad'. Recent research into psychosis and spirituality suggests an essential commonality of quality of experience between the two, and that polarization is limiting.

WALKING THE THIN LINE BETWEEN OPPOSITES

The edge may be created by the tension between polarities, between the opposites of dark and light, of day and night, good and evil, masculine and feminine, sun and moon. The extreme tension of the edge may be challenging us to meet the opposites we hold inside or outside and find a third position or transcendent function for the extremes. For, when two energies are polarized, nothing can happen and no life can flow. Some of us emerge into adulthood believing we can only be either X or Y. We are either perfectly in control or making a terrible mess. While we may have survived by our rituals of control, over time, the lack of balance will begin to bother us. Our control rituals may become more severe as we begin to fear them slipping. Or life may plunge us into a 'mess' where we have to get our hands dirty and face all the fear this entails. We journey then at the edge until we find a 'third' position which is not either–or, but which moves us into a closer homoeostasis with the qualities held polarized as extremes.

THE EDGE AS THRESHOLD OR LINK

The edge is also a threshold in the way that the beach is the threshold between sea and land. Gates, doors, porches, vestibules are all thresholds. When we step over the threshold, we pass from outside to inside, or vice versa, from one place or state to another. Some thresholds are wide and spacious, like the great marble vestibules or decorated anterooms of eighteenth-century stately homes.

Thresholds may have a very thin edge, feel flimsy, like the flap of a Bedouin tent, the small entrance to a rabbit burrow, and be without lock or key, fanfare or watcher.

Some thresholds are accompanied by watchmen and women, by guards or servants, by janitors or jailors. The keeper of the threshold can be a figure, like Janus the Roman god of the portal whose two faces look both in and out. Other thresholds come with uniformed attendants, soldiers or prison warders, doctors in white coats bearing syringes and electric-shock treatment.

Whatever its distinction, the purpose of the threshold is to create distinction between one place and another, and to name formally the process of passage. We talk about being 'in transit' when in between countries; we are 'in passage' while moving through the in-between phases of life; we are 'in transition' as we experience change. We move into the anteroom before entering the room of our destination; we enter the 'post' period, after an experience, as in post-natal depression, post-traumatic stress disorder.

'Falling over' the edge or 'off' the edge quite suddenly when not looking, or when doing something else, speaks to our experience of the edge in an internal sense, when we are plunged from one state of being into another. The threshold then is absent, or hidden perhaps within events which preceded, which can only be seen clearly with hindsight. Many people who are thrust into a spiritual experience or a Kundalini awakening feel their bodies taken over by a powerful physical sensation. Others speak to falling in love; being caught by a psychological complex or archetype. Then it seems as if we are taken over by the forces of fate. The speed of the experience is a vital ingredient in the process, giving us no opportunity to turn back. We are pushed onwards into the journey, with neither time nor hesitation to hinder us.

There are other passages, where the threshold seems to be endless grey monotony and we are kept waiting, seemingly in limbo, feeling in suspense, with life on hold. Others may be via the passages of war, being sent to another country, away to school or university, through a relationship, religious experience or a threshold crossed by death.

The threshold has been well marked in our literature and in art. For example, the sentimental carrying of wife by husband over the threshold of shared home symbolizing his ownership and strength over her passivity. Jacob's ladder reaches up to heaven from the ground with its myriad of steps, both threshold and journey in itself, but also a link between the earth below and the Divine. For Dante, the gates to hell, immortalized by his poetry and the paintings of William Blake were signposted

Through me is the way to join the lost people . . .
Abandon all hope, you who enter!

And once through, accompanied by Virgil, 'with a face so joyous it comforted my quailing' began one of the richest and most moving journeys recorded.

Religious structures may honour times of crossing the threshold as in bar mitzvah, Ede, in baptism, confirmation and wedding in the Christian church, in taking refuge in Buddhist tradition.

Inner thresholds, such as between girl becoming woman and boy becoming man, the biggest change we as humans make biologically, are marked by the passage of puberty and adolescence. For many cultures, this threshold is honoured by rites of passage which include rituals and initiation ceremonies with dancing, fire, chanting, special clothes. Masai warrior mothers shave their sons' heads. Samburu warriors leave their mothers for isolation and bloodletting with other males to mark the threshold between boy and man.

THE VALUE OF THE EDGE AS THE PLACE OF CHANGE AND TRANSFORMATION

At the edge, we are caught in the liminal space, the moment in between, between where we have come from and something new beyond. We are in an unclassified place. The edge carries the tension between what has gone before and what is to be. There are often no safe places, no boundaries, no classifications to help us define what is happening. We are thrown onto the suspense of the unknown.

This is a challenge. Just staying with the unknown nature of this liminal place without wanting to change it is a huge step. It calls us to be truly in the present moment, with whatever there is. This may mean a difficult feeling, a painful memory or image. We are being invited to be a different kind of explorer than before.

Naming ourselves as travellers in an alien space can help dignify the process as we learn, by the collection of our many one steps, to be the most creative of travellers.

We may need a shelter, a bridge, a boat or vehicle to help the crossing of the edge. We will need an attitude of unconditional friendliness to ourselves; and the hand of loving kindness.

Taken alone, the edge can seem a grim and hostile place, our dreams and inner life prey to murderous forces and evil giants. We may face the terror of believing ourselves to be on the edge of annihilation, lost, abandoned, in the void, alone forever, doomed to bite the dust and travel like Pilgrim, or Adam and Eve, expelled from the green Paradise Garden to walk in dirt and dust, or to crawl naked and wide-eyed unable to sleep, like Nebuchadnezzar.

When we have become accustomed to the demands of liminality, which forces us to look within, we may see how much we have divided our thinking and attitudes into 'either–or'. It is these divisions that create edges in the first place. Within them we notice our attitudes to right and wrong, there or not there, being and doing, fair and unfair, nice or nasty, happy or unhappy, what we feel we can and cannot do. Surrendering to and bearing the liminality of the edge means moving our attitude from a system dominated by dualistic thinking and into the wider spaces that begin with our concentration on the present moment.

Witnessing and bearing these aspects and our attitude to them moves our experience of the edge as only a frightening limited place to a place of initiation where we are shifting from one level of self-understanding to another. Our feet and hands become accustomed to the climate and landscape of edge including the fears we have of falling over. We may walk on and see what has been awakened during our time on the edge. We may see the edge then as creative threshold. We may simply find that edges hold less fear for us and that we have more space inside. However long it takes and whatever the nature of the struggle, we will have forged a bridge between known and unknown, and our steps will encourage others.

Our journey throughout this book is to explore the very nature of the edge we find ourselves on and any future edges we may encounter. Some people teeter about on the edge for fear of going over it into something worse than what has taken place before. Some freeze upon the edge. Others plunge over the edge in desperation.

Our images of the place may change as will our range of feeling. The emphasis is upon creative map-making even when our only guide is the idea of a slim thread or a distant light or lamp in a dark landscape, which someone else may be holding for us. However narrow the line, dim the light or alien this place it is of ultimate value that we learn to tread slowly. As we may pay attention only to that which is right before us, we see more, we may even find fresh lenses. Then the edge becomes the forging place, the place where new inner dimensions inside are created. Often what seems new, and lessens the narrow tension of the edge is simply accepting the old in a new way.

2

Naming Our Individual Edges

When we say 'I'm all on edge', or 'I'm living on the edge' we are often describing feeling cramped, tense, limited, stuck, and all the feelings that accompany this – anger, fear, anxiety. This state of being on the edge may last only a short time, a day or week, or it may hover for months and years, even a whole lifetime. The feelings will vary in intensity. What lingers is usually a longing to be relieved, to find a solution and get off the edge as soon as possible. For all of us find it very difficult to remain in a 'no place, going nowhere'.

It may take time before we recognize being on an edge. All we know is that internally we feel 'edgy' and short of space. Externally something may be going wrong, decisions must be made and we cannot attend to them. We often try to rationalize our situations by trying to attach them to some event. We may believe our edginess is connected to our not being able to get over a particular loss or relationship. Perhaps we have been feeling physically unwell and have tried many approaches to feel better. We may have been trying many solutions to bring about change. Being given a reason, diagnosis and suggestion for concrete solution, or the label of an illness for which there could be treatment can bring temporary relief. The 'mid-life crisis' is often used as an overall metaphor for the 'edge'.

FEELING OUT OF CONTROL

When we start to feel out of control for no apparent 'reason', we tend to cling onto what is familiar, however old and worn that habit may be. If we have to cling on for a long time we begin to lose energy and contact with anything meaningful. People speak of feeling 'cut off' from anything of beauty or meaning as their world narrows through fear. It's as if then that we are captives to our old ways, only able to peek through a tiny crack in the fence or wall that we feel hems us in, at life outside. Some describe their experience of the edge as being like a slave on a vast ship on a swirling sea, in a car whose brakes have gone, or imprisoned in a cage or fortress where they could only imagine normal life going on outside. When we feel trapped and out of control we long for freedom, to link with something that makes us feel at home to ourselves. Beauty and poetry, song, dance, fun, pleasure, the inner music of our soul seem to elude us.

On the edge, we feel unable to relax, use humour, let go into any form of pleasure. The great censorious hand of fear holds us back. We may find ourselves postponing: 'I'll wait until . . . When . . . then . . . '. As we smell the fear of lack of control, we tend to try to assert control in the ways most familiar to us. We may seek control by not allowing any feelings for example, so we shut down all close contact with others. We might try to think our way out of things, making more and more lists, demanding more and more letters, memos, making unnecesary phone calls, trying to 'read' or 'think' our way out of fear of the unknown. We may try to work harder physically, if this is what we know best, believing that once a certain goal is achieved we will feel better. But the opposite tends to happen. We feel as if we are running faster and faster, but our world is getting narrower and narrower. And as our anxiety and levels of stress rise so our actual functioning and performance drops. We may feel like Sisyphus doomed to push the boulder up the hill for ever more.

Many of us in this place are trying to use will-power alone to keep going. There is the fantasy that *if only* we can assert ourselves in the *right* way, go on for long enough, everything will fall into place. We may find ourselves secretly relying on magic to bale us out. We may be drawn to fortune tellers, psychics, that will offer instant cure. We may find solace in alcohol, drugs, driving very fast, we begin thinking of a way out of our dilemma. *We begin to court unconsciously the crisis of the edge to bring about resolution.* But sadly, the force of using constant will-power pushes us into our left-brain hemisphere, eclipsing the right hemisphere which is responsible for our ability to relax, play, recuperate and make appropriate judgements. So the methods we feel compelled to try when on will-power alone do not serve us. In fact they exacerbate our situation. And often, this is all we can do because it is all we know how to do. Even those of us who 'know' these things find ourselves spinning and running at certain times.

LOSS OF CONNECTION WITH INTUITION AND SPIRIT

Intuition and spirit can be hard to reach when all our energy is taken up with surviving the narrow ledge of the edge. It's as if we just cannot let go, or take any risks.

We can begin to recognize that intuition and spirit are eclipsed by asking ourselves when we last felt joy, experienced real pleasure, or were drawn into the soul of music, poetry and dance for its own heart's sake.

Recognizing and naming being on the edge can give us just enough ground to take a step back within ourselves. This step back – probably the most important one we take in this process – allows us a margin of space. In this space we can connect with an inner observer, who can become wise and compassionate to our process. This space may also allow us to refresh our intuitive powers and to take up the thread of spiritual practice.

All spiritual paths begin with an experience of going out of control. In Dante's *Divine Comedy* he writes:

Midway this way of life we're bound upon,
I woke to find myself in a dark wood,
Where the right road was wholly lost and gone.

In the section devoted to working through the aspects of being on the edge, we will be exploring how contacting our own wise guide or observer can take us through the journey we must

31

make, from dangers of the edge to the edge as a threshold for the next part of our journey. It is in making the movement in attitude from clinging on to what is habit because of a fear of falling, to choosing to jump that we gain control over what feels as if it has control over us.

COMMONLY SHARED FEELINGS OF BEING ON THE EDGE

The above includes the following.

- Feeling as if 'nerves are all on edge'. Images of being skinned.
- Feeling 'in limbo' or as if suffering a 'terrible waiting'. Images of being sentenced.
- Feeling constantly afraid, or in dread, as if something terrible were about to happen. Fearful images of impending doom.
- Physical tension in the neck and shoulders and in our back, chest, and down our arms. Images of being in a vice, crab claws digging in.
- Disturbances in breathing, such as breathlessness, holding breath, hyperventilation, not getting enough breath. Images of lack of air, longing to be high up in the air.
- Persistant headaches, nausea; images of hammers in the head, lead ball in stomach.
- Fatigue, exhaustion. Treadmill images, man in the box, running for a moving train.
- Sleeping poorly, waking frequently, or sleeping heavily waking unrefreshed.
- Appetite changes. Overcontrol of food such as feeling obsessed about eating. Not eating by forgetting to eat or avoiding eating.
- Minor physical difficulties such as poor digestion, constipation, menstruation problems, sprains, twists, back pain, stomach irritation.
- Accidents ranging from scraping the car and twisting an ankle to collision and fracture.
- Confusion of thoughts, unable to think clearly, and accelerated thinking.

- Obsessional ideas and thinking. (Ruminating compulsively on one word or idea.) Obsessional thinking can be seen as the result of unmanageable feelings taken up by our minds, in order to try to sort them out, but creating an *ideé fixe*.
- Paranoia is a medical term used to describe a state of unreality. The word derivation is from *paranoos* which means literally 'mind always preoccupied'. When the edges feel rigid, as in some states of paranoia, we fall into the grip of believing literally our paranoid thoughts or fantasies. When the rigid edges are challenged to become more dynamic, we are able to hear our voices with a poetic ear and not take them or act upon them literally. Then we are able to take relief from the incessant edge of demand that paranoid moments inflict upon us.
- Feeling desperate, despairing, wanting a way out, feeling suicidal. Images of death.

So far we have identified general associations with being on the edge. Next, we are going to try to identify, through the use of our imaginations, the images that dominate this alien landscape of being on the edge. This will give us a starting place.

1 We use our imaginations.
2 We explore through the imagination the feeling of the image and what this might mean to us.
3 We begin practising remaining present with what we find.

IMAGES OF THE EDGE

All of us have visual images. If asked to imagine a green field in summer we can see it in our mind's eye. We may also be able to feel the warmth of sun on our skin, smell the clover or honeysuckle in the warm summer air, see a bird or butterfly resting on a buttercup. We can also probably feel the atmosphere of the green field and be able to see the quality of the grass, its length, strength, lushness. There may also be other images that come to us in this field that come of their own accord, without being suggested, like water, for example, or a mountain, or sheep, cows.

Before words, the world of the image was prime in all our lives. The touch, smell, feel, sound of our inter-uterine and nursery years are all recorded within us as images. The touch of a hand for example is an image. It may be amplified to become the soft embrace, a firm holding or a fierce slap. The hand will be the hand of a person who has meant something to us. We may also carry this image and seek to find it metaphorically, such as wishing to be held in a cradle of care during times of loss and bewilderment, or the longing to be held by the embrace of the Divine. Images remain unconscious until triggered by something happening in our conscious life; a conversation with an old friend about schooldays may bring into consciousness an image of the schoolroom, or the voice of a teacher, the smell of school dinner, the memory contracted into the stomach wall of taking examinations.

Images may appear to us in dreams, and come charged with feeling and animation that do not allow us to forget or discard. The image of the cliff edge, the well, the waterfall, the bridge, the mountain pass, the chasm, the dark pit, the cage, walking a tightrope, falling from a parachute, at sea with only a tiny life raft, suspended above a high trapeze. Variations of these images have been shared with me by people who have identified feeling on the edge, and who felt that the visual image connected them in feeling and meaning with that place.

Images serve us well because they come from the place within our imagination that is not contaminated by will. Images are universal language. They move us from our small individual struggle into the wider world of symbols that connect us with universal images. These symbols and images speak to us every day from the outside world and often collective images have the power to release in us great feeling. Images of the huge soulful eyes of the children of Rwanda needed no words to speak to us, but became symbols of innocence trapped in slaughter. Images of the dignified procession of robed Kurds making their weary, hungry way into the mountains of Kurdistan having been hunted out of Iraq after Desert Storm became the powerful symbol of unfair marginalization and invited depth of feeling. And so it is with the symbols of hero and heroine, prince and princess, magical saviour, potent advocate.

Living on the edge invites many different images. There are general images of *The Wasteland*. Our individual wasteland will have its own images, geography and attributes. The following images may help to illustrate the kinds of feelings that help us identify being on the edge.

THE PRISON

Images may be of a box or coffin or cage. We feel trapped or cornered as if we have no choices. We are experiencing a time of confinement and limitation where our freedom is curtailed. This may have come about through actual imprisonment where we have been found guilty by law of a crime. We may have been forced to flee our own country and feel imprisoned in a new country as a refugee. We may feel imprisoned by an illness, by a relationship, by being unable to cope with the demands of others. We feel under sentence and if the sentence feels unfair, harsh or punishing, then we are likely to feel crushed and punished. If there has been unfairness, we may also feel impotent rage. We might feel shame and guilt for being in this situation.

Imprisonment makes us face ourselves, our fears, our deeds, our true beliefs. Prison may make us more of a criminal because we learn more deeply the criminal ways. Prison may make us a hero, like Nelson Mandela and Václav Havel who learned to speak about true freedom by serving their time in places that represent materially the opposite of freedom.

Even when we are imprisoned we can be free.

Thich Nhat Hanh writes about his monks being imprisoned in Vietnam and Cambodia and using their confinement to develop their meditation practice. They emerged fresh and alive. He writes, in a talk given to the inmates of the Maryland Correctional Institute in the USA, 'For me, there is no happiness without freedom and freedom is not given to us by anyone; we have to cultivate it within ourselves. By freedom I mean freedom from afflictions, anger and despair. Every step you take can help you reclaim your freedom.'

THE TIGHTROPE

Images are of being on the high wire like the acrobats at the circus. There is only the grip of our feet through which we have to keep our balance. All our attention is fixed upon an imagined spot in front of us. We are unable to look to left or right. There is nothing to hold on to any more. Images of falling are also present.

We feel as if we are treading on eggshells, we feel limited, tense, tight, we hold our breath.

Feeling our feet and finding enough balance for a moment helps us to ponder on what our tightrope is connected to on each side, or, who is holding the rope we have to dance upon. The two positions in opposition to which our rope is attached may remind us of other times that are symbolized by the images of a balancing over a chasm. Is this a split within ourselves, or a split within our family, work or relationships that we are trying to hold together?

Is our current life finely balanced between two extremes, two opposites where we believe we have to make a decision but cannot?

We can hover forever like a fragile hummingbird, feeding intermittently, or we can concentrate upon walking to one side in order to view the other. As we realize the power of the image to reflect polarities within our life – jobs, relationships, attitude – we may allow for a third position to emerge. Whether we stop long enough for the tightrope to become a bridge between two aspects or for a new position, we need to stop and gather energy, and to move within the unknown space over which we are hovering.

THE DESERT

The desert landscape is dry and dusty. It feels as if we are to walk on the hot sands forever. We are constantly frustrated by being lured into relief by mirage, and having the fruits of our hallucinations as our only companions. There is no moisture in our life and we feel dried up, thirsty, boiling hot by day and cold at night with only dust and sand as our companion. It's as if we have to remain present with our dryness while being teased by the false longings created by our mind. We have to endure and walk alone, find ways to breathe more easily and make a journey to find a true watering hole, a true oasis.

This desert feeling may occur when we have stayed in one place, physically or psychologically, for too long and the energy has gone out. Nothing seems to grow any more. We feel alienated, marginalized, alone. It may be the experience during depression or after loss. D. H. Lawrence talks about 'a long difficult repentence'. We bite the dust when we are rendered down low. Images may also be of being left on the desert of the moon.

Only time in the desert allows us to reap the harvest of this place. In this time, we learn about life without the element of water. We meet the desert creatures, camels, Bedouin riders, jackals, or no one at all. We have to find ways to water the needs of our own soul that are beyond the mirage. We have to find ways of 'slouching toward Bethlehem to be born' (Yeats).

THE VOLCANO

The volcano is an image of the power of terrifying destructive energy for those who live in its shadow. Images are of fire coming out of the earth, streams of molten lava, sudden eruptions, a red mass breaking through the earth completely out of human control.

A sense of 'living on top of a volcano about to erupt' may symbolize feeling constantly angry or smouldering rage. It may be that we've been bottling up rage or blurting it out inappropriately as in a tantrum or flinging fury at others. It's as if we've been boiling away for a long time without knowing of this energy within us. Perhaps we've had earth or water heaped onto our fire and had to keep it hidden and buried. Perhaps we've never appreciated our fiery nature, perhaps been afraid of it and now it has come to claim us. Perhaps we have been in a situation where our fires have gone cold.

Acknowledging the smouldering volcano means recognizing

37

the depth of fire within us and learning to understand its power. Acknowledging the volcano has erupted means we are in crisis and the molten lava of our inner self is on its own course. We must feel the release of its blow, operate a damage limitation exercise to the regular lands of our being. When the fires have died down, we have the quietness after the explosion, a change for mourning and reparation. And we have the newly cleared grounds paved by the path of molten lava, which become fertile and productive as we address them.

THE CAVE

It's dark and damp, it may be within the earth with stalagmites and stalactites, or part of the sea coast involving the smell and sound of the sea. It can be like a womb, or an alchemical flask where all life gestates. We can feel safe, but in an alien place as if we are vulnerable and sheltering for a while like the hermit crab looking for a new shell. We can hear only echoes and move around tapping walls and smelling things but nothing is very clear. We are accompanied by the creatures of the cave – insects, snakes, bats, nesting birds, or there may be bears, wolves. We are like the hermit and in this place we have to make friends with those creatures or elements that have been shut away or repressed. We are visiting parts of ourselves that we hid or locked away a long time ago. At first we will be only frightened. It's usually dark in caves and smelly. We can liken it to a period of gestation where something has to be out of the light and protected from the outside world in order to reveal itself to us and we to it. We may learn to respect our cave and return to it from time to time out of choice.

THE CLIFF

Images may be of a steep precipice over a chasm of unknown depths. They may be of storm-swept sea cliffs, surrounded by rocks. There may be only rocky precipice, available only to gull and fulmar. We are stranded, as the popular saying goes, 'between a rock and a hard place'. Will I remain stuck hanging in the wind, pecked by great birds? Will I fall and crash? Will I fly or learn to jump?

We are between the danger of the rocks and the wateriness of the sea and sometimes there is beach in between. The cliff is a place of great drama in all stories and movies. In our own psyche, it can represent the threshold between known – dry land – and unknown – the ocean. Cliffhangers are times when everything hangs in the balance. We are often at the mercy of fate or nature that shoves us into the next phase. Months of tension may have preceded being in this place, or, we may court cliffhanging experiences in our life as a way of creating excitement and drama. Many situations in life create this kind of atmosphere today, especially within areas of urban work. Did he jump, or was he pushed?

In this place, we may make all kinds of promises to ourselves not to get here again. But only by recognizing ourselves in this place can we learn to be familiar enough with our drive and anxiety to befriend them rather than be ruled by them.

THE SWORD

Feeling 'cut'. Cut to pieces. Sore, cut down to size, belittled. Feeling as if the sword of Damocles is hanging over us. Feeling the sharp blade of a tongue, having a battle. Having to get our sword out to fend off an enemy. Bleeding.

The sword is also the vehicle we need for cutting through illusion and old thinking. The sword of truth awakens us to the reality of our predicament. It can hurt and we can feel the blood rush of relief. It may be that someone has spoken to us with blade-like wit or precision and we feel cut by the sharpening of their tongue.

How do we stay with our sense of wound and not get into self-pity? How do we embrace the surgery and allow it to heal us? What is it that needs cutting away and what needs to emerge? Who are our helpers and guardians for the time of healing?

The sword is a powerful image for discrimination. We need a sword to 'cut the crap', cut illusion and get to the point. We need to understand fully the power of the sword and use it wisely; when it is of greatest service to us and to others. Using it wisely requires us to be flexible, in balance, non-partisan. It requires us to be in practice like the great samurai, breathing in and breathing out. In the wrong hands it is a weapon of war – intellectual or of body. In wise hands it becomes the illuminator, the dibber making a passage in the ground through which the seed may grow.

THE NIGHT SEA JOURNEY

Here we are literally 'all at sea'. Awash, surrounded by water, by the ocean swell.

We fear our boat is too small or we have no boat at all. We have lost the oars, the sail is broken, we are adrift on a huge sea of the unknown. We might be swallowed up by a huge whale and have to live in its belly, like Jonah. We've lost our bearings and are tossed around by something so much mightier than we.

Using images to address the feeling of being all at sea helps us to anchor our experience enough to ask 'what do I most need in this place?' The most obvious answers are a life-raft or lifebelt, a passing ship. These give us something to hold on to gain balance. We may have to look up at some point instead of using all our energy just to hold on. This may help us to see the night sky and there might be stars. Psychologically, when we look up, away from absorption in the ego, in ourselves, we see other galaxies.

We might have to learn to swim, to negotiate with fish and whale in deep water. We will certainly become familiar with the element of salt water, bringing us into the depth of our own feelings, awash with emotion, the salt of our grief, the reality of being human in a world of oceans. Just surviving is our first call. As we become familiar with our new element we may learn new skills: to become divers, for fish, pearls, buried treasure, we may have to find psychic water wings, or develop our own internal lifebelt.

Margaret had as her image of being on the edge standing alone on a ledge near the top of a high cliff in a freezing gale wearing only a thin cotton dress. She was standing holding onto some scrub grass afraid that the ledge would break and there was nothing between the ledge and the ocean below. She had always been terrified of water. She had not learned to swim and hated to get wet. She believed that if she fell into the water she would either be drowned or dashed against the rocks. To help her secure her position on the cliff face, she imagined a pair of fulmars who had made their nest nearby. They befriended her and helped to secure her to the ledge by building it up in strength, so that she could stay as long as was needed to make a decision about her position. She was very fond of birds and they had come to her rescue at other times. Fulmars are a loyal and protective part of the gull family and can scale height and soar great escarpments without flap of wing. This gave her time with safety to look down into the water below. When she looked more deeply at the nature of water, getting wet, feeling water all around her at risk of being pulled under into an ocean depth, she began to weep. She associated her weeping with a huge ocean of feeling inside her belly. In time, she connected this ocean feeling to the loss of her mother when she was aged 4. She watched her aunts weeping while she sat dry eyed as the 'good little daddy's girl'. She had made this division early on by deciding to be the controlled good girl who never cried or had deep feelings for fear of being in the nowhere world of feeling and washed away. What had taken her to this place she felt was the ending of a long relationship with a lover. The relationship had been dreary and out of energy for some time, but neither had been able to end it. They were unable to mourn for the loss of what had gone and move on. She had felt suspended in the relationship for the last two years until her partner had one day announced that he was about to move in with someone else. It was totally unexpected and the next day she was left with a half-empty flat, which was too big for her, and a terror of falling.

Once she was able to work with her image, she was able to begin to get just a little wet with feeling and to allow herself, with help and containment from therapy, to be awash with the unresolved grief for her mother, as well as her most recent relationship. In connecting with her true feeling, giving it value rather than living in dread of it, she was able to let go in other feeling situations. A feeling connection then enriched her inner life as well as her communication with other people.

One man experienced his edge as being a narrow path hemmed in a dark valley in between two rocks. The edge was long lived as he struggled with the melancholy of depression, with the dark of despair, while he accepted the shadow of the mountains either side of himself.

> Late, by myself, in the boat of myself
> no light and no land anywhere,
> cloudcover thick. I try to stay
> just above the surface, yet I'm already under
> and living within the ocean.[1]

WORKING WITH IMAGES OURSELVES

Find a quiet place and settle with pen and paper and see what comes to you when asking the following:

1 What is your image of being on the edge?
2 What is its geography, landscape, feel, smell, sounds?
3 Is there anyone or anything there with you?
4 Does this image remind you of anything?
5 What does this image tell you?

Let the image itself offer you information from day to day. Let it tell you about itself. Allow yourself to have a dialogue with it, checking in every other day to see if anything has changed. This need not be hard work. Think of it as a way of checking blood pressure or temperature. It is in fact a reordering of the situation of your innermost life.

The image we have of being on the edge will hold much information about different aspects of ourselves, the place we find ourselves in and the journey we are to make. As we look into it and contemplate it more deeply, we will find dimensions we had not considered before. Take for example the image of the humble onion and the spiral this creates. If we were to have the

---

[1] From *The Essential Rumi*, translated by C. Barks with John Mayne, Harper (1995).

image of an onion, we might think it a rather ordinary, basic and somewhat dull image. The following steps could show us a different picture.

Focusing

Look carefully at the onion in the image. *Your* onion. Concentrate upon its details, the actual size, shape, colour, smell, texture, the setting in which the onion is placed, the time of day, the light around it, anything else that appears in the image. Any detail we can bring to the actual setting in which our image is placed helps to bring it more sharply into focus. This process is like focusing the lens on a special camera that will show us the depths of something.

Sticking with it

Stay with the feeling of holding the onion. Here we just pay attention to the onionness of the onion and what it is like to be close to it. We just remain with this and see what happens. Where that closeness to the onion might take us.

Personal association

Then we move into pondering on our personal associations with the image, in our example, the onion we have now focused upon in minute detail. What is this onion like for us, what do we associate with this image? For example: it makes me cry when peeling; I use it in all cooking, it adds flavour to things; makes my breath smell; it grows in winter in my neighbour's garden, or at the railway allotments; I don't like onions much; my gran had a bun like an onion. These are our first impressions and personal associations with the image of the onion.

What does the image remind me of?

If we were to ask: when were you first aware of the onion?, we might evoke a memory such as helping gran to peel an onion to make a stew; wielding a spade on a frosty morning to help mum to dig them up in the garden; carrying a bag of onions home on your bike; seeing a French onion seller with a string of them on his bicycle; uncle Joe's prize onions at the vegetable competition; harvest festival onions; the street market and baskets of onions; being shown the number of inner rings within the onion when it is sliced open, the pinkish flesh when the outer wrapping is stripped away, counting the rings, dipping half an onion into ink and making a print for a birthday card. And each of these reminders from the past will carry an evocation of feeling. I felt sad, happy, in awe. I heard singing, sighing, the robin; I was alone, with others, with an important person for me; and, deeper in meaning, this was the first time I had been allowed to help, to use a knife, to do something on my own, perhaps even the first time I saw a grown-up cry.

Amplification

Here we look at the symbol of the onion shape in a wider context. We see it is used in the sacred domes of mosques and orthodox temples, it is a central Indian design. It is often seen as a symbol of unity, the many in the one, the cosmos, as a symbol of revelation, peeling off layers to reach the centre; is used to help baleful lunar powers in pagan tradition. It is also a root and linked with the earth and all the qualities of the earth as it grows silently within the dark of the earth's womb.

If we stay with whatever has emerged from this short four-point exercise, what kind of information emerges? In applying this knowledge and awareness to our own individual life, what does this mean for us? That we are being invited to inspect the image of the onion and its layers, perhaps seeing and naming the different layers until we come to the actual core or heart inside? What is the heart or core that we are being asked to meet right now?

3

Maps of Being

Most of us don't think much about what it means to be a human being in this life until something happens to make us question it. Why this? Why me? It's often when things go wrong or feel very difficult. Only when encouraged to take a philosophical or spiritual attitude do we reach below the surface of everyday events and emotion. Even then, if our spiritual attitude is caught up in a rigid structure or dogma, it can be very hard to get beyond the edges of things being right or wrong, good or bad.

Religion and psychology have produced several different maps of being and we may have been born into a family where these maps are very present. If they work for us, then we are supported by their rituals of rites of passage and are connected to familial or ancestral systems. But when there is spiritual impoverishment we grow up with no maps of how to be other than ways governed by the progress myth of doing well. This is often composed of urban consumer dreams in terms of gaining power and money, being successful in the eyes of others, achieving external goals, having objects that reflect us well.

Gaining skills and knowledge, building homes, having children are all important aspects of living. The analytical psychologist C. G. Jung thought that the tasks of the first half of life are connected to strengthening an ego with which to live in the world as we find it. This thinking is also reflected in the eastern philosophies based upon Buddhism. We 'need to be somebody before we can be nobody'. This means that we need to have developed a good enough sense of ourselves in order to be able to surrender it within the discipline of a spiritual practice and thus go beyond the limitations of ego consciousness. When we try to attempt a spiritual practice without having been grounded in reality we can experience inflation and disintegration.

When we try to live a life based only upon a myth of getting somewhere that will make us feel better, we tend to live in the past or in the future, we feel spiritually impoverished, and our attention to what is going on within the present moment is limited. All spiritual practice begins with placing our attention on the present moment as the object of our mindfulness.

Many people arrive at the edge because of both soul and spiritual hunger. This may take the form of yearning, and longing to 'come home' to something long left behind, that heralds a step to connect with what has gone before and give it meaning, what C. G. Jung and James Hillman call soul making; what other psychologists have called entering the 'un-thought known'. There is also the sense of being starved of connection to the rituals that create a sacred space, and to a system devoid of judgement and limitation but open to the breadth of the present moment, to wisdom and compassion, to an ever present truth.

Our dimensions of soul and spirit cannot be fed by an ego which is too fixed or rooted to being in charge, by external achievements and possessions. All the money and external power structures in the world cannot meet the place of the soul when it cries out for love, and the spirit when it seeks to rise and connect.

1 *We create edges in order to survive*
2 *We dissolve edges in order to become wise*

Trying to create maps that will help us to understand and bear the edge, we can call upon two different but complementary ideas. One is the idea of a journey. We come from somewhere and we go to somewhere.

The other is the idea of there being nowhere to go, no journey. In the latter, we use our attention to remain exactly where we are and not try to change anything.

46

The journey indicates a path, the path we have already come along and which has influenced the person we are: from birth, through childhood, adolescence into adulthood and the path we are undergoing along the edge. In the next chapter I have mapped this current journey as carrying many of the hallmarks of initiation.

The 'no journey' involves learning to be mindful of every moment and step we take, to be truly present with our feeling, with our body, with our attitude and the constructs we place upon ourselves and others.

These two steps carry two different purposes for us as we explore the place of the edge. The maps of the journey of initiation help us to gain a working understanding of where we might be in order to stand still enough to remain present with our experience. Remaining present with our experience is what really transforms the edge from being a place of random chaos and ambivalence to being a place of potential transformation and spiritual emergence. When we leave attachment to the personal – 'all about me and mine' – we allow a spaciousness. This 'standing aside from the personal' offers us the possibility to become near to and witness a transpersonal dimension, which allows for another attitude. This is a space which widens as we practise. It is the place within us; the island within ourselves that we return home to every day; the place no one can ever take away from us because it is our practice and ongoing relationship within it that is in our care.

JOURNEY: PSYCHOLOGICAL MAPS OF DEVELOPMENT

Life is unable to be lived by any of us in a linear, preprogrammed way. It is not a logical progression, like an academic timetable. Human beings evolve and journey throughout their lifespan, cultivating, processing, inhabiting, culturing different aspects of themselves according to the forces that come both from without and within. The analytical psychologist C. G. Jung believed that at the point of the quickening of life inside the womb, was a DNA seed within the growing foetus of a unique individual self. This unique self is connected to both the personal life of the human family with its biological genes and social and cultural heritage, to an individual myth, and also to the collective unconscious. In order to survive and communicate in the everyday outside world, each individual needs to develop a container called ego through which the individual personality expresses itself, and within which the developing self is protected while links between the ego and self are strengthened. A strong, healthy ego structure helps to hold and withstand the powerful energies of the inner self especially when it makes links with the larger, collective force of the self, for Jung, the closest we get to an experience of God. It is through the work of the ego that we are able to make images conscious and connect with their variety and meaning. When the edges of the ego become too rigid and we live only in that realm, we become too fixed and limited, cut off from the inner connections that help us grow wise. And if the edges of the ego are too undeveloped they can be weak and porous and we may be flooded with unconscious images and feeling forces which sweep us over the edge of conscious containment as in schizophrenia and psychosis.

Reaching maturity and wisdom demands an inner journey that promotes the flexible dance between the ego and the self. This journey moves through the early childhood and adolescence stages of ego strengthening and development, through adulthood to a mid-point of life where the differentiation between ego and self is at its most extreme. The 'mid-life crisis' frequently heralds a call to step aside from the demands of ego consciousness into a new space, a space from which we may develop wisdom and compassion, from which a commitment to spiritual practice may begin to take the place of earlier 'gods'. Today, many people are reaching this 'mid-life' crisis point in their late twenties, and again in their early forties.

At any point in our life, we can be awakened to a different drum beat that heralds an opportunity to contact another facet of our true nature and purpose. The homoeostatic principles of the psyche operate to keep us moving and to not settle for a compromised 'little' life.

Maps help to give us a guide as to where we might be heading and help us to see where we have come from. If we were to fall into an alien place and not naturally know the geography, a map gives us some bearings. The map is not the country and however complete the map it always carries the thumbprints of the map-maker. It may take some time before it makes any sense to us personally. There are however certain landmarks that are so outstanding they are unquestionable. In external geography, the ocean, water tower, forest or main highway, are clear markers that help us to locate ourselves. Birth, childhood, school, friendships, deaths, illnesses, siblings, home, travel, university, children, marriage, relationships, jobs, are all landmarks in the life of an individual and will all carry unfinished business.

Psychology has offered many different maps over the last hundred years to help travellers make sense of their inner landscape and the journey they might make throughout one lifetime. No one map can encompass the complex structure of a man and woman's personality and life span. Professor Charles Tart in a recent presentation said that western psychology had majored in understanding 'endarkenment', studying what goes wrong for humans in terms of neuroses and psychoses and looking backwards rather than forwards. In the East, millions of people have as their goal of life 'enlightenment', the hope of awakening, of being reborn into a more auspicious rebirth. Psychology tends not to refer much to maturity other than modes of acceptance and adjustment to the status quo.

When we place the word spiritual next to maturity the words we use as description are: a deep sense of calm and peace; an ability to remain present within a storm; being able to be alongside others in a sense of presence; holding the capacity for deep listening and healing; leading a life committed to ethical and contemplative practices that refuse excess; a leavening sense of humour; no dogma or piety; the capacity for true joy and happiness; leading a life committed to humility, simplicity, compassion and to sharing fellowship and love.

BEGINNING THE SPIRAL OF LIFE

As we contemplate the journey of life, the image of the spiral serves as an illustration of the way life keeps returning us to similar places. To our individual myth, path, our way, our karma.

The spiral's constant weaving round means a movement on and away and up or down but with a centre that remains constant. It remains a constant focus to come back to as we evolve, and as the spiral demands our movement into and around the core. The spiral may swing wide when we feel we are separate from the core; it may bend deep into the core when we are pulled again into our deepest innermost places.

The interface between ego and self is the place where unconscious and conscious aspects of life meet. The interface is the stage upon which the drama of our psychological life is played. Here at the interface we meet our dreams and fantasies, archetypal figures, images from the soul life, calls from the spirit.

Infancy and childhood

From before birth, self and ego are merged within the body and the unconscious world of whoever was mother for us. We may have had an actual mother, or a stream of different mothers, or father, uncle, grandmother, sister, may have acted as mother for us. But whoever took on that early role played an important part in shaping our experience of ourselves and of relating. No other period of brain learning and physical growth is as significant as this period. Human beings emerge at birth as more helpless than any other being in the animal kingdom and their early years after birth are crucial to their development. The task of these years is for external independence to take place: walking, sleeping, eating, the physical command of body functions, language mastery and communication skills. Internally, we need the ego to begin to emerge in its own right by the time we go out into the world of other people and school, and for a sense of being real to take root within us. Whatever is our own true nature will always try to assert itself, our traits, likes and dislikes, our gifts, pleasures, capacities, our ease with our own body, our expression of feelings, our way of thinking and our connection with a transpersonal dimension. These different aspects will be seen, perhaps noted and commented upon by others. This is important because it means that we are being mirrored by others. We hope to be mirrored as we really are, not as others wish us to be. Too much mirroring in another's image can send us looking endlessly for our real reflection in all the wrong places. But no mirroring at all leaves us unseen, as if we did not exist.

Our sense of being 'real' may begin to be consolidated during these years as we extend our time of play and growth, develop different skills, make friends and take our place within the family. Or, we may have to hide being 'real' because of adverse circumstances which ask us to create edges inside. Whatever climate we find ourselves in, our capacities get sharpened because of the demands of outside life. We may find, in looking back at old childhood photographs, that we see something of our real, original selves in the little figures, before the mask of adaptation hid us from outside view. Some people are able to connect with images of 'otherness' that began during childhood. A special image or imaginary friend or place, a sense of presence, a particular connection with nature, with stones, rivers and birds, with trees and plants, with animals, with an imaginary inner landscape, with a favourite toy, an object, a dream.

If something stops the path of our natural growth, such as early separation, bereavement, or when we experience a restricted or conditional, cruel or abusive early life, we adapt accordingly. This arrest creates a wound, often resulting in a separation from or rejection of our own true nature. At some time in the future life, this wound will draw us back for the purpose of reparation.

EARLY-LIFE IMAGES

The edge often produces images and feelings that remind us of early life. A sense of helplessness for example, or an inability to express ourselves in words. We may feel childlike, as fragile and unprotected as we once felt when very small, or we may feel persecuted, trapped, judged and discriminated against, as we once did early in life. And, while these experiences may be actual, it is important as adults to address the feelings these experiences bring with them that live on informing the decisions and choices we make in our daily lives.

51

The wound that Margaret suffered over the loss of the mother had remained unaddressed until her adult relationship ended. None of us can go back and undo what happened to us and we cannot spend our lives looking for the perfect mother or father we never had. But we *can* become kind and wise midwives to ourselves, going back in time to heal old wounds and making a conscious decision to choose not to be limited by what has gone before. We can use what has happened to us to link up with our individual myth and archetypal pattern, so that we grow in our wisdom and understanding and widen our compassion. Those people who are now awakened to their wound of abuse from childhood are doing so amid a collective awareness of the fact of childhood abuse. There is the opportunity to be alongside with understanding others and address this wound. Then there is the choice of attitude as to how this wound is carried. We can see it only literally and seek literal and legal revenge. We can put it all away for ever. Or, we can mobilize our shock into a wider embrace of all the suffering, which spreads back into generations of family secrets. This demands us to open our hearts and minds to the depths of what is possible within the human family and bring it from its darkness into light. It could also move us to pay attention to all our negotiations and relationships so that they move into the realm of the power of love, rather than the love of power.

ADOLESCENCE

This is a time of emerging ego when it needs to be strong enough to withstand the great changes going on within, and the call to move away from parental bonds and find apprenticeship with the clan in the outer world. In adolescence, we often begin to hear more loudly the earlier drumbeats of our own nature and begin to connect consciously with our individual myth. This occurs at a time of great pressure from outside to conform, to grow up, to take on the challenges of the world, to develop an identity in order to appear in the world and the world of work. We often take on paths at this time because of immediate need rather than reflective attitude. It is a time when new tunes are being tried out alongside the pressures to either *do* or *be*. The interface is between an emergent sense of self and authority – mentors, heroes, special people and relationships of the tribe or clan. This is a period of great experimentation, of intense feelings of death and rebirth. The rituals of this time are those of the peer group, the campfire, music making and exchange of talisman and dress. It is a time for the parental influences to drop back. It is a dangerous and exciting rite of passage when the longing to get high, to find a transcendent self, to get above materialism and into idealism and flight are at their most compelling. The ego needs to be strong for the emerging self to express its values. And the depths of experimentation can seem extremely dangerous today. To push to the edge of parental limit was once to stay out late, drink too much or get your ears and nose pierced. Today, finding an individual edge away from authority can involve joyriding, crack abuse, stealing, killing, as if the imagination has taken wings and gone beyond itself in the literal sense. For all these adolescent excursions and diabolic routs, what is it that is being imagined, hoped for, transcended?

ADULTHOOD

Here the ego and self can be furthest apart. We feel split in two. It is as if the ego has grown as much as it can, fulfilled its tasks and now the energies of self move into prime position and begin to be heard in the most compelling way. Crises of ego/self differentiation always include an experience where the ego begins to experience death. Since we feel our life through the ego, this can be extremely shattering. It may be an actual death which takes us to the edge, or the threat of death, it may be the death of an important relationship, a job or belief in a cause or a deeply held faith. We may fail at something which is death to the ego and for a while we may feel we are lost in the darkness not knowing where next to turn.

This point of feeling the ego so completely separate from the inner self may be arrived at earlier, when we feel alienated from anything meaningful but yet do not have the strength to cope. When we have held all life's energy within our ego personality this part of us can become inflated. It begins to think it has all the answers, that it is God himself. This is a dangerous situation because the energies of the self are powerful and need a strong but humbled ego with dynamic boundaries through which to transmit its numinousness. The transpersonal psychologist and philosopher Ken Wilbur, writes that a spiritual journey requires a strong ego to withstand the power of the self with its numinousness and invitation to meet the brightest of lights and the darkest of places.

Maturity seems to be connected to being able to live in the present and relish every moment, not constantly running into the future nor dwelling on the past. There are sadnesses rather than regrets, acceptance rather than resignation, a half-full glass rather than one which is lamented as half empty. We know the limits of our own ego and its tendency to try to rise up and we deal with it with humour, maybe bashing it down from time to time or laying it to one side so that other elements may rise, either within us or in younger people around us. We have accepted that we are simply not in charge and surrendered ourselves to the 'way' sometimes seen as a higher level of consciousness, at the same time as holding the thread of what has been important in our life and for our own individual journey. During maturity we move into a deeper sense of what is important for ourselves and for others. In looking more into our community, into life, we can move into positions where the wisdom that comes from the heart, from a love of life, begins to sound a note for all sentient beings, for communication and harmony, for peace and the end of suffering.

WOUNDING

When we live on the edge we are closest to our woundedness and our fragility. All of us are wounded in some way by what has happened to us from our life so far. There may have been actual and obvious woundings along the way that we know about and can identify. Or, our sense of 'real' is compromised by our having to be something other than we are. Many of us can identify how we carry a sense of woundedness within our body – we hold our hand at our throat, we draw in a breath, we rub our stomachs, arch our backs, we press the palm of our hand onto our heart. Words, situations outside, smells, feelings, sound, and simple questions asked in kindness can press us on this place. We may not know its full nature until the spiral of life passes over it. This may create a mere flutter, or press hard and feel too close, threaten to open up the wound or plunge straight at it.

How we carry our sense of woundedness matters. Accepting the wound, making it ours rather than someone else's fault, means making a relationship with all that we are. This can bring relief. To know that some things really are difficult or impossible, and it's not just our lack of will-power. To accept woundedness and start from there frees us from having to search endlessly for 'perfection' – whatever that is!

Sometimes we can get caught up in imagining that a relationship with religion or therapy will cure all and we will return to innocence, to the Garden of Eden that we imagine childhood should have been. Or we may spend years looking for the mother and father we never had, but in the outside world rather than inside ourselves. Relating fully to what has happened to us means allowing the expression of the wound in all its blues, purples and reds, and finding healing ways of addressing the wound. This may involve many different kinds of relationships with others and with reading, with making sense, looking for understanding, and letting go of an overattachment to our identity as a sufferer or therapy junkie.

Woundings may also connect us to our individual myth, and in a wider sense to the familial and archetypal patterns which will be constellated throughout our life. The latter may be referred to as 'karma' in Hindu and Buddhist cultures. Karma is a useful concept meaning archaic remnants from other times, the baggage, emotional, physical or actual from other experiences. When karma 'ripens' we experience a mixture of our wounded-ness, our shadow side and the intense feeling that another hand is at work in our life. When we work through karma, or we forge a new understanding when we are brought to the edges of ourselves, we leave it behind in that particular form. We may well have to encounter it again as the spiral of life presses us on both our wound and our individual myth, and each time we have the opportunity to deepen our understanding.

SHADOW

Shadow means 'that which is not in the light'. As we become conscious and stand in the light, our light throws a shadow. Knowing the nature of the shadow is part of our psychological and ultimately our spiritual practice. The shadow of a human personality is composed of all the aspects that have been unable to be recognized. There are always shadow aspects, and to be cut off from our shadow is to be alienated and one dimensional, it is to see shadows everywhere, in others, in world leaders, in our own worst nightmares. Peter Pan is unable to be himself and truly 'free' to stop flying around until Wendy sews his shadow back on.

The shadow often provokes fear and misunderstanding. It can be judged as something bad. It can be personified when we say 'oh that's my shadow talking' after we've been rude, using it as an excuse for lack of real awareness and responsibility. In some spiritual groups, there can be a tendency to deny the reality of the shadow and search only for the light. Any psychology, religion or system of meaning that does not make space for the shadow encourages it to fester and grow bigger in the darkness. The whiter we make Christ in Christian cultures, the blacker becomes the devil. The more we put energy into being 'good' and sharpen our swords against bad, the more likely evil will be manifest.

The Breakthrough hexagram 43 of the I Ching reads 'If evil is branded, it thinks of weapons, and if we do it the favour of fighting against it blow by blow, we lose in the end because thus we ourselves get entangled in hatred and passion'.

Perhaps it is getting easier for us to take on board that as humans we have within us the capacity for both good and evil because evidence of darkness and what collectively we have called evil is so manifest in our world. Fighting tribe against tribe in Rwanda and Yugoslavia; capture, rape and torture that goes beyond current time but about which we are now having to make a clearer view. It is not new that human behaviour can be cruel and evil, but we have now so much documented evidence that it places upon us the responsibility of choice, to not take these paths. Some of the events that have come to light over the last ten years have made us face just how dark human beings can be. The Aids epidemic forces us to be mindful of our sexual practices. The evidence of widespread child sexual abuse within families and religious orders force these dark practices into the light, as does having to take on board the fact of child prostitution.

After the mindless massacres at Port Arthur and Dunblane and the murder of James Bulger by two ten-year-old boys we try to look for causes, and to find justice for the victims. These events uncovered individuals who had been marginalized by society. Unlike the travellers and Gypsies with an identified poetic and symbolic role and place among us, these loners find no place to go other than into the deepest recesses of their dark tortured minds and act from that place.

Within us the shadow is like a great compost heap, full of discarded matter as well as unknown depths. It both festers, and in it grows the new. It is through connecting with figures, feelings, aspects of the shadow that we are most likely to grow and become wise.

But the shadow is not just for integration. It is to be respected as a dimension that always sobers any idea we might have that we've got it all together. Wholeness is accepting both sun and shadow. When we live on the edge, we are closest to our personal darkness and most vulnerable to the shadow figures who may beckon us from their shadowy places and even take us with them for a while, into the depths, into madness, into behaviours that shock and appal, repel and seduce, into the places furthest from the light. And it is in this place that we get to know our darkest nature best and we develop an appropriate awe for the energy that has come calling.

CAPACITY FOR SOUL MAKING

The word soul is used widely throughout the world, in and out of religious context. When something really touches us in the heart we truly become aware of it. It is, in that moment, meaningful. Human beings have the capacity to make a meaningful relationship with suffering. Those moments when life and people really move inside us are soulful moments. Choosing to embrace the possibility of soul making means that we deepen our life from random event into related experience. Music becomes 'soulful' when it touches us deeply and carries with it the voices and experiences of its creators. Poetry often speaks directly to the soul experience. It moves right into the heart bypassing the intellect. In his painting *The Scream*, Edvard Munch speaks to the souls tormented by pain and loss. A nation can seem to be suffering a 'soul sickness' as in the tearing apart of Yugoslavia and Rwanda.

It seems that profound human experiences touch us on a soul level, inviting us into something beyond our everyday awareness and control. Opportunity for making connections with soul is everywhere and everyday, and usually connected to something quite simple. The worn suitcase we use daily that we inherited from a grandparent. A vase of flowers filled by a child. The eyes of someone stripped of attachment to control through illness. The deep soulful look of a faithful animal.

Soul can easily become eclipsed by the everyday world when we are rushing about to get somewhere, catch the bus, fix a meal, earn money, fight with each other. But soul is still there, and it is always, as James Hillman writes, 'in the thick of things, in the repressed, the shadow, in the messes of life, in illness and in the pain and confusion of love'.

MEETING OF OPPOSTITES

Many of us emerge into adulthood with a divided sense of our choices of how to be. We feel we must be 'either–or' and 'if–then'. Throughout this book, we will be looking at different aspects of polarized choices and how we can move into a third position that does not split us in two and leave us stranded on the edge of tension between the two. Also, dualistic thinking maintains suffering. It hardens the ground around our potential for spaciousness and spiritual emergence

One of the most troubling polarizations in human life has been that between the qualities of masculine and feminine energies. Jung referred to masculine and feminine as the archetypes of animus and anima, widening the context in which we approach them, way beyond the gender issues of male and female. The creative spark of yang (animus) is brought to life by the containment of yin (anima). Each need the other for any creative form, their archetypal energies are vital for the creation of life. All life is dependent upon the uniting of masculine and feminine. A revisioned relationship of these two has particular importance today as we are moving from the historical dominance of masculine consciousness into a realignment with what is feminine. This realignment is crucial for the global development of listening and relatedness.

SUFFERING

All life involves suffering. How we approach the nature of suffering makes a great difference to our ways of bearing and transforming it. If we harden down onto suffering by identifying ourselves with it, we become a victim; if we put all our energy into seeking to blame, we become bitter; if we try to disappear into suffering as an escape from reality, our suffering will increase.

Bad things do happen in life and will continue to do so. There is no way of avoiding suffering and Buddhism embraces this with the first noble truth which recognizes that 'life is suffering'. But there are ways to be within suffering. Suffering is often perpetuated by our attitude, by our ignorance, by a refusal to let go of a belief that underpins our suffering. Beliefs such as 'it shouldn't be like this' mean that we are holding on to how things 'ought' to be. The suffering which puts us closest to the edge is our overattachment to order, to the rational or to blame as an explanation for our suffering.

When we suffer, we are in dialogue with ourselves, we are in the 'mess' of feeling and confusion. In accepting this we have places that allow us to be alongside suffering, to be wise and compassionate in this place. This may be all that is needed to bring us into a new awareness of how we are within our suffering. This small step gives us a space. It lessens the rigidities that perpetuate suffering. It also allows us to proceed to widen the space around suffering. In this space we allow for a transpersonal witness. This is an experience where we are in the presence of our reality as a human being, engaged in a life where suffering is involved, and we are also beyond being identified with that suffering. For many people this place is nourished by meditation or other spiritual practice. It becomes the ground within which we grow and heal and our relationship with the divine in all nature is manifest.

PSYCHOLOGICAL MAPS

Psychological maps are helpful in that they help us address our personal history, what happened, where, when, how, and what we have brought out of it for ourselves. Psychology charts and maps patterns of behaviour that are learned and thus can be unlearned with the light of consciousness, practice of awareness and the companionship of a therapeutic relationship. Psychology also offers self help, as it suggests specific self-monitoring, self-awareness, and gives us ways of doing this alongside regular feedback. But psychology itself tends to be limited in its approach to the philosophical realities of suffering and im-permanence. Many psychologies are based upon a medical model of cause and cure. They look backwards in time to the roots of difficulty in the past, and each different psychology has its own understanding of health and wholeness. If psychology only looks at individuals as being the sum total of their given psychological labels, neurotic, psychotic, paranoid, anorexic, it leaves behind the individual traveller and mythmaker with his/her own context, story and unique thumbprint, as well as the creative capacity to stand still within the demands of suffering and find ways to be.

The result can be an emphasis on replacing one set of responses with another, more 'socialized', which may be helpful, but it may not give us the means with which to remain present with the fact of suffering. Understanding the roots of neurosis and maladaptive patterns of behaviour are important and helpful. Depth psychology helps us to become part of the drama of our own history and life, and to give it meaning on personal and transpersonal levels. The focused therapies, especially cognitive analytic therapy, help us not only to name and understand our story, but to name and challenge the learned patterns of behaviour that have helped us survive but need revision if we are to be free of their hold. A further step is to find ways of being alongside the whole of our emotional life, our pain, our past and present suffering that allow us a real relationship with it, not distancing ourselves from it, as in analysis of 'why?' And not disappearing into it by emoting or catharsis.

TRANSPERSONAL PSYCHOLOGY

Transpersonal psychology draws upon many psychological traditions in order to understand the development of a person, and uses an integrated approach in its practice of psychotherapy. The main departure point from other psychologies is that its core values include and honour the 'spiritual' dimension of human experience. It also draws upon the structures and maps born out of the meditative disciplines of the East and West. It draws upon Buddhist philosophy's understanding of the nature of suffering as contained in the four noble truths: first, the 'reality of suffering'; second, that 'suffering can be overcome'; third, the 'analysis of suffering'; and, fourth, the practices we may develop to overcome suffering.

The word transpersonal simply means 'that which moves beyond'. An experience of transpersonal energy refers to those experiences which move us and allow us to see beyond everyday consciousness which is the domain of the ego into a more spacious realm. Everyday experiences of beauty, awe, wonder, numinousness, light, peak experience and out-of-body and psychic phenomenon, dreams, near-death experience, breaking down to break through are all examples of experiences that go beyond experience dominated by personality alone. They include but go beyond the everyday 'I'. Transpersonal experience allows a bridge into states of experience where we move beyond suffering, and sometimes, into glimpses of what Ken Wilber calls the 'basic open ground', out of which, as he understands it, all life flows. In recognizing our capacity to have transpersonal experience we may become open to immanent and transcendent states associated with the higher consciousness, and in the deepest, darkest aspects of our being when all consciousness has been given up; when we have broken down and given up.

Transpersonal Psychology seeks to nourish the human capacity to make the two steps. Both into deeper personal meaning and also those spaces within us that are not limited by personal experience, but free from suffering. This means finding a way to be alongside suffering without being identified by it. The moments when we enter these spaces extend our experience of the wide canvas of life experience.

A transpersonal perspective is not limited to psychology. It can widen our listening capacity and our heart and mind connection to many different concerns of life. In a recent article in the *Psychologist*, the journal of the British Psychological Society, David Fontana and Ingrid Slack write:

> At all levels and in all societies, transpersonal experiences and beliefs can affect human relationships, life philosophies, reactions to death and bereavement, education, and responses to economic hardship and natural disasters. A major feature of transpersonal psychology is its conviction that the psychologies of the Eastern and Western worlds have much to offer each other. The scientific approach of the West, with its emphasis upon objectivity and exploration turned outwards, and the contemplative approach of the East, with its emphasis on self exploration, have the potential to cross fertilize each other in a number of important areas.[1]

NO JOURNEY: SPIRITUAL PRACTICE

Being open to a transpersonal dimension means being open to all life containing both sacred and profane aspects. Our attitude becomes flexible. We practise remaining in the present moment in order to be fully aware and awake. We learn to be truly present with the reality of our feeling, however full on that may feel. In remaining present, we become observer and observed of our

---

[1]   Fontana, D. and Slack, I., *The Psychologist*, June 1996.

experience, we are at one with it, we are not analysing, saying this is my mother complex thus distancing ourselves from it; and we are not avoiding, repressing saying 'I'll think about this later'. We see the sunrise and are deepened in awe; the song thrush calls to us at 5 a.m. and we are awakened; the cry of a child who has lost his mother pierces us and we are present with his devastation; the shuffling steps of a blind beggar whose shoes are made of rags moves us to simple compassion. We are not identified with sentiment or pity, we are not trying to analyse or sort anything out, we are simply present. Spiritual practice is very simple and direct. We may practise in our meetings with others, in our daily work, with our chores and tasks. As we step, in practice and connection with the potential for spiritual dimension, we may come to be aware that there is a rhythm and order to things.

We may nourish this practice of awareness by the regular practice of sitting meditation or mindfulness practice where our breath, a sound, walking or what we eat is the focus for our practice. In Buddhism, there is a saying that 'we already have all that we need it's just that we don't see it'. In developing the practices that allow us to be present in the moment we swing less between thoughts of past and future, usually dominated by a wish for things to be different or seeing our life as a means to 'get somewhere'.

We can be enriched by a sense of spiritual presence, spiritual awakening, meaning, reaching out to others. We are humbled to take note of all that happens to us and to the invitations life brings to take us to new further understanding.

Divinity, whatever its theoretical base, is here seen as an abstract state which is none other than where we are in the here and now. We do not have to go anywhere.

REMAINING IN THE PRESENT MOMENT

The starting place for spiritual practice is *not knowing* and *not trying to go somewhere*. This means that we remain present with our experience, in the present, exactly as it is. We follow the flight of a bird and enter into that experience, watching our tendency to try to identify the bird and recall the last time we saw such a bird. We remain present with our emotion. Not trying to analyse it, change it in any way or avoid it. The focus of our mindfulness is simply the attention to exactly what is happening now.

The edge itself – meaning any edge of being – is rejoiced in by eastern cultures and in the transpersonal psychologies and the psychology of C. G. Jung because it epitomizes *not knowing*. This is a state of being that reflects the potential for true emptiness that emerges from giving up attachment to event or outcome. This state of being makes it possible for spaciousness, for entering into states of wisdom and compassion. This does not happen easily but by being in all the states referred to as 'properties of the edge', surrendering to them and allowing their edges to dissolve. It is our relationship with the properties of being on the edge that creates a new relationship within ourselves, a new kind of freedom.

SELF-AWARENESS AND SELF-PITY

Self-awareness

All we can ask of ourselves is that we grow in self-awareness. Being self-aware is not being self-conscious. When we are self-aware, we know something of our blind spots and what situations, people, events are likely to trigger them. We cannot know everything, but once we have fallen – and we will – into a no-go area, all we can ever ask of ourselves is that we are aware of the process that has gone on. In many situations, our regular spiritual practice helps to nourish our awareness of all life processes. We are less likely then to be mindless rather than mindful. Self-awareness may be a by-product of having been on the edge, because it is at the end that we must really learn to see clearly with all our senses and wits so that we may continue walking.

Self-pity

Operates when we attach to a difficult feeling a mental construct or idea that makes that feeling worse. For example, when feeling a sense of loss, if we construe – 'they have done this to me' we add to our feeling of loss, anger, blame; we become a victim. In doing so we move away from the feeling itself, so we are no longer present with our feeling of sadness. In moving away from the pure river of our own sadness, we enter a jungle territory of feeling a victim – revenge fantasies, getting even, making someone pay, telling others of our unfair treatment, gossiping, building a whole world of woundology. Staying with the pure river of sadness, we may feel overwhelmed for a while, awash, drifting along or caught by a tidal wave. We get wet, we taste the salt of tears, we swim, we sink, we tread water, we are bathed, we find fish, we get a wave inside our mouth, we have an experience of sadness that links us with all other sad people, we join humanity in its suffering.

The edge invites us into self-pity at every step and in every feeling aspect. We have a choice to recognize it, and to feel it when it grabs us and to separate ourselves from it in order to experience our feeling fresh, just as it is. When we do this, our experience of feeling changes because we have entered it.

MAITRI

This Buddhist term may be defined as unconditional friendliness and loving kindness to oneself. Maitri is a necessary ingredient to beginning our spiritual practice. When we sit or walk for long periods of time with only the content of our mind to do battle with or deal with, we need to bring in this dimension of kindness to ourselves. This means we stop allowing self-judgement and self-criticism to dominate and undermine our early steps.

Throughout this book, as we look at the journey, on and through the edge, we will be journeying with a transpersonal perspective. My hope as writer is that each reader will find what is their own transpersonal note within them and begin to connect to this note for it to be the soul caller and guide throughout all of life. As a general guide, the hallmarks of a transpersonal perspective are listed below.

1 To attend to each moment and the note, feeling and image it brings forth.
2 To listen with the inner, poetic ear, inviting the artist to paint the inner landscape in images and senses.
3 To learn to be flexible, to dance to the music our soul is making as we experience it in ourselves and recognise it within others and the world.
4 To know that everything has potential for meaning, the meaning that we give it even when we cannot fully see it at the time.
5 To know the difference between the voice of the ego personality and the voice of the self. To connect equally with both and to become aware that both are part of a spiritual and soulful journey. That a meaningful life and spiritual journey is not limited to religious organizations or to a life lived in spiritual isolation.
6 To know that solitude is necessary for the development of listening, but relating is necessary for growing, and that love, beauty, laughter and joy are food for nourishing the soul dimension.
7 To make an offering to the wider, greater transpersonal forces and energies that move within us and around us so that this link is kept aflame.
8 To go very very slowly so that the nature of the edge may reveal itself to us freely, without our attaching to it meanings before what is due.
9 Making the edge a place of potential transformation of attitude.

4

Paths of Initiation

Because the edge is such a difficult place to navigate there will be many moments when we think 'what is the point?' Our knowledge, the limitations of ego consciousness and the ordinary levels of conscious awareness are not up to processing such a potentially major change in our being as the edge is offering. When something else is clearly afoot – and we know this because we will have tried all our known mechanisms of coping with change – we have to enter a period when we find ways of surrendering to the process that is going on, but which feels 'not of our own doing'. Our questions have to move from 'why me?'; 'why now?'; 'what have I done to deserve this?'; 'it's not fair!'; 'now I've blown it!'; to: 'what is this [experience] saying?'; 'what does this [my feeling now] serve?'; 'who can I speak to about this?' Or, simply, 'please help me, whoever is out there'.

These times mean that 'not knowing' or 'having to know', is more important than knowing where we might be going.

Our relationship with the many dimensions of not knowing, of stepping aside from systems of control into transpersonal space is what is in potential. We cannot create this experience without an edge and all the aspects this creates. We must journey in the dark and as we do so we develop different ways of seeing and sensing, we hear sounds we hadn't known of before, smell new fragrances, meet the figures that live in the dark that have something to tell us.

There will be times when we will actually give up trying to process our way through it as conscious brave warriors and long for the relief of unconsciousness. This may involve trying to lose our pain and misery in some mindless pursuit – drugs, drink, television, sex, shopping, oblivion. When we can no longer be vigilant, we have to make resting places within our edge. Sometimes we get lost for a while, and then take up the conscious thread of the edge path again.

Any offering we can make to this in terms of recording and working with our dreams, keeping a journal of our random thoughts and feelings, working with the images that draw us into the non-rational levels of awareness, will all help nourish the thread of awareness we are trying to create.

Throughout this book, we will be describing the edge as having the potential for profound inner change and for the transformation of one way of being into another. The overall metaphor for this journey of the edge is initiation. With the metaphor of initiation come structures that allow us to name and make sense of the different aspects of the journey and give us permission to engage actively in their meanings. Then, our modern resting places, or culs-de-sac, are entered into knowingly, not blindly, and can take the place of the initiation rites that were once a vital part of the structure of human social life, giving a shape and a dignity to the passage from one state or way of being into another. The fact that we may not see this process until we are caught up in it or beyond it does not matter.

HEARING THE CALL AND SEEING THE THRESHOLD

An example of the 'seeing' that often heralds the initiate's journey comes from a man I saw during a period of crisis who suffered from terrible boils; they kept appearing despite countless courses of antibiotics. He felt that he was being punished like Job for something he had done but was unclear what it could be. He experienced that suffering of depression and exhaustion into which we can sink when we have nowhere else to go. He felt what was happening to him to be unfair, unjust. In his bitterness, he felt compelled to drive on, overworking, unable to rest, and fixated all his nervous energy upon a need to have revenge for his life's losses. Part of his treatment for the boils was to take a salt bath three times a day, to let the salty water bathe his back and buttocks where the worst crop of boils were living. He had to buy common salt in large quantities and prepare his baths. Then sit in them for fifteen minutes each day. He thought: 'this is what *she* has brought me to' referring to his ex-wife, and he commented on the bitter taste his wife's leaving had left in his mouth and what suffering this had caused him. The salt baths involved a laborious procedure, one which grounded him, but he complied with it, like a dutiful martyr.

Then one day he mentioned how the salt had glistened as he measured it out and how amazing it was that such a simple common substance was his treatment in a time of highly sophisticated antibiotics. When asked what the salt baths meant to him, he replied thoughtfully, 'It's a bit like some sort of ritual isn't it?' Then the naming of the ritual and what it might be preparing him for awakened his curiosity. It became the thread that took him further in investigating the ancient properties of salt itself. There is the salt of the earth, he would say about those friends who were supporting him. He began to read about salt, about it being an ancient substance that links us with all the elements, that is vital to life, the balance of the salts within the cellular structure being key to molecular life. He read that salt was an arcane substance, associated with sea water and the process of baptism, and he was encouraged to read Jung and the alchemical writings on the subject of salt and the saltings.

What came out of this for him was his need to examine the substance of bitterness. He had been left by his wife, who had gone off with his best friend, and he was crazed with grief and jealousy. He had thrown himself into work in his own business, exhausting himself, eating badly and getting drunk at weekends. He came to see the boils as signals for something trapped, angry and poisonous locked inside him. He became more consciously aware of his consuming bitterness and desire for revenge, how much his drive to get even by taking out fury and destruction on himself could cost him dearly in terms of relating. As he caught its reality on the wave he became more in touch with a much deeper level of grief for the loss of his wife as a person and the marriage they had shared and some of the quality of the things he wanted from intimacy with another. He saw that the boils had alerted him to a choice: he could become like the closed angry weals of his boils – septic, full of pus and fury, erupting and raging at the unfairness of fate and losing himself in his wretched bitterness (the expression 'to lose oneself' is useful here, because we 'lose' the hold of our ego selves in order to know that which is beyond ego); or, he could engage in the salty process of self-preservation (salt is also a preservative), by expressing all that he felt inside about the loss of his wife, to wash the wounds and cleanse them by his daily baptisms, to weep salt tears for what was lost and to begin a process of intimacy with himself. This movement – from bitterness to acceptance – and the ensuing wisdom to be gained he saw as his personal initiation.

In *Mysterium Coniunctionis,* Jung writes: 'bitterness and wisdom form a pair of alternatives; where there is bitterness wisdom is lacking, and where wisdom is there can be no bitterness. Tears, sorrow, and disappointment are bitter, but wisdom is the comforter in all psychic suffering'.[1] Just this movement, from the tunnel vision of revenge, to seeing his boils as a symbol of both his distress and the departure point for a new relationship with the self, allowed him to change the lens on his struggle to that of an initiatory journey.

He was being offered both a way to *be* within the actual situation, and a way forward and choices. And the process seemed to be directed to a complete change in his attitude to relating, both to himself and to others. His movement was from the position of holding on and controlling that which he desired, to opening the way for the true expression of his own feelings in relation to himself. Ultimately, he made the shift in attitude from potential bitterness to wisdom.

---

[1] Jung, C. J., *Mysterium Coniunctionis: An Enquiry into the Separation and Synthesis of Psychic Opposites in Alchemy*, Routledge, p. 183 (1963).

NAMING THE EDGE AS AN INDIVIDUAL
INITIATION PATH

The journey of the edge involves many extremes. The qualitative aspects are described in Part Two, the pitfalls in Part Three. In Part Four we look at developing the images, threads and the stepping stones that offer us a helping hand as we stumble and weave our way, sometimes for a period of years. We can see that our experience of the edge carries within it initiatory processes where the individual initiate undergoes the tasks, tests and the waiting common to all initiatory journeys. The basic pattern of initiation is departure; initiation (comprising death, a passage and rebirth); and finally the return. The actual naming of the way of initiation is important. This may be named as such by someone else, someone who knows us and perhaps has an idea of where we have come from and are going to. Or, it may be a wise person, a priest, an older person such as grandmother or friend, or it could be a teacher, therapist, group leader. In *Forms of Feeling*, Robert Hobson quotes from Joseph Conrad to describe the moments of seeing and naming: 'My task which I am trying to achieve is ... to make you hear, to make you feel ... it is, before all, to make you see. That – and no more, and it is everything ... that glimpse of truth for which you have forgotton to ask'.[2]

Moments of seeing, insight and naming come in simple ways, when we are not trying or expecting anything. They might arise from the woman who hangs her washing in the next-door garden; or someone speaking on a background radio. Whatever awakens us to an awareness of initiation, this process is of huge value. When we accept this path, we shift to be in readiness for it, instead of fighting against it. Once named, we have a blueprint that helps shape our experience. We surrender to it, and we create and connect with a thread or light to keep hold of as the going gets tough.

In the process of initiation, we become the hero or heroine setting out on a quest and we take on the gravity and enormity

---

[2]   Hobson, R., *Forms of Feeling: The Heart of Psychotherapy*, Routledge, p. 115 (1985), quoted from Conrad's *The Nigger of the 'Narcissus'* (1897).

of such a venture. To accept our edge as such a path means dignifying the process and joining forces with all the other heroes and heroines that have come this way. We will not be alone. The words and images of others who have been this way can guide us. They will not be exactly the same, for modern-day initiations are about the time we are in, but they will have many resonances with the mythological and historical figures who have left us their words and footprints.

Dante, seeing an unknown figure as he stumbled about, called, 'Have pity on me whatever thou art or very man or ghost'. His figure turned out to be the poet Virgil who became Dante's guide through the first two stages of his journey, until Dante handed him over to Beatrice with the words: 'Now let pleasure be your guide'. We may meet internal figures who speak or whisper to us in phrases or words that puzzle. And these all form threads that we take into the labyrinth of the journey of the edge as we accept its initiatory task and take this into our own hearts.

The idea that this journey is about something and can have a creative or positive outcome because of what we make of it during the travel can deepen and strengthen the thread that carries us through. However flimsy the thread and however many times it gets lost, it is none the less as vital as the thread Ariadne held for Theseus in the underworld. The people that name this thread or light our way as we stumble along become our wise elders or talismen and women, those who know something we don't yet know, or have been on their own initiatory paths and can shine their light on ours. These people may well be everyday people we meet only once, or in passing, or they may become firm friends and guides. They speak with the knowing of those who have travelled far, and their language is seamed with the wisdom that is enough to ignite our imagination.

The gift of true wisdom is that it does not tell anyone what to do or how to do it nor does it speak in literal terms as if this were this and that were that. The musical tone sounded by the wise friends we meet at the place of the edge will outshine anything we have known before because their quality will resonate with the music of our own being. It is at these times that, if we are open to receive it, people, stories, images and examples of those who have travelled before us are the beacons in the dark, the footprints in the desert, the friendly hand coming into the well, the kindness among the harsh rocks. And there are also those figures in mythological or world history who have described being on the edge as an initiate's path and recorded their journey and findings for us to read as our turn comes around.

STAGES OF THE INITIATION PATH

Initiation, put simply, means the act of origination into the new. When we initiate something we start, open, get something going. To be an initiate means that we place ourselves within the process of learning something new and follow a custom or ancient practice that has been recorded throughout the ages. The initiation journey we have been looking at in this book concerns the invitation from the edge to become mindful and conscious of what we are doing and to turn away from the pull to remain unconscious in order to individuate into the sacred purpose of our life. The goal, or outcome, is wholeness. Wholeness means embracing all that is within us, and without, with an open heart. It means dark and light, sickness and health, knowing and not knowing. The processes of initiation will all be individual but having a blueprint for the initiatory journey means that we are able to share certain ingredients and follow a well-trodden path.

The call

The way of initiation will vary and the thresholds are many. The call to adventure may come from a chance event, a mishap or disaster, a blunder or mistake. Some of us are initiated into a new relationship with ourselves by a relationship we make (like C. S. Lewis), by following a religious belief (St John of the Cross), by being prepared to embrace all suffering (Siddhartha, the Lord Buddha), by a programme of study (like in the film *Educating Rita*, where the process of academic learning moved Rita away from her old life into something new). We may be called into initiation through a long illness, such as Elizabeth Barrett Browning, by an accident, or a near-death experience.

We may have felt tense and unhappy for a number of years and know that something is wrong but be unsure how to name it. We may simply feel that we have outgrown the set of personality clothes we have been wearing and need to discard them to move into others that represent the next phase of our being, or of our life.

In ordinary biological development we make a progression from childhood to adolescence, adulthood. Each of these stages are entered through a process of initiation, where we let go of being a child for example and put on the uniform of school, entering the school gates for the first time in our new shoes. As we move into adulthood and take on adult responsibilities, we leave behind the robes, rings, music of that long rite of passage – but, let's hope, not quite completely! Yet in all initiations something has to die in order to give space and life to something newly developing. And this is particularly so in psychological and spiritual growth. The Zen master will pour tea for the student who seeks enlightenment and continue pouring until the tea spills over the cup onto the floor to illustrate how we must become empty before anything can come in. We must let go of what we have become attached to and is now redundant, in order for a new attitude to emerge. James Hillman writes: 'it is illusory to hope that growth is but an additive process requiring neither sacrifice not death. The soul favours the death experience to usher in change'.

Most of us are called to become initiated into carrying out different tasks such as the movement from son or daughter to adult, parent, grandparent; from disciple, acolyte or handmaiden to teacher or leader, from innocent abroad to mature responsibility and engagement with life. Those who are unable to accept the call to initiation can feel stuck or in limbo, living only from a childlike or adolescent aspect and feeling cut off from the wider, deeper experiences a relationship with the inner life can offer.

The call to become awakened to the opportunity of moving beyond the known, beyond our woundedness into a wider experience may come gradually, or, we may just wake one day like Dante, and feel we are in a dark wood where all is wholly lost and gone. Some may call this depression, or mid-life crisis, or even psychosis, but whatever it is called we have the choice to enter into it as an initiatory experience. It may be some time before we move into seeing it in that way. When we do, we will have crossed from one side of the river of life to the other, and our geography and our needs will be different.

Feeling lost and in alien territory

The first stage seems to be losing that which has been familiar and finding ourselves in alien territory. Then there is the process where everything that has gone before does not work any more.

The tendency is to try to hold on, to find a 'cure' especially today when many cures are on offer. We may have to make many detours and experiments in terms of approaches to what might be the nature of our suffering or strange new condition. But we tend to end up alone, having to make the best we can with what feels like the worst of ourselves and use the resources that only we are able to recruit and which work for us. We make the stumbling way on alien territory where we learn as we go. During this process, we often meet benevolent figures who are protective and give us something to guide us. Dante's Virgil appeared only when Dante surrendered to being 'wholly lost and gone'. Inner figures from dreams, figures that come to mean something for us from literature, nature or actual figures within our life. They may be animals such as a magic hedgehog or frog, a butterfly, a figure which carried almost supernatural powers to help us on our way when we are lost. Later even to help transform the old into the new.

Crisis

When we step over the threshold something of our sense of self dies. We tend to be 'plunged' into crisis when things happen suddenly. But we may also realize that we have gradually been sliding closer to actual crisis when some of our habits or patterns are mirrored back to us. One person said to me:

> I hadn't realized how I'd been neglecting my body until a friend stayed with me and I had only stale food to offer her. I was shocked – and so was she – to face this. I had been totally preoccupied in keeping myself going each day to the job I hated that all my energy was spent. Her visit prompted me to ask for some leave so that I could address just what was happening to me physically. Of course this meant getting into my feelings, all the feelings I'd put on hold. But the crisis initiated me into quite a different attitude to self-care, and to giving time for feelings to come in.

Crises usually involve extremes such as accident, emergency, bleeding. Internally crises only tend to occur when our store of knowledge or wisdom runs out and we are in a completely new place, when we simply have no more reserves to call upon to help guide us. A crisis represents both danger and opportunity. It is internally that feeling of being in something new and alien where nothing that has gone before can be called upon to help us to cope. The danger is that we will collapse ourselves into this place. The opportunity is for something new to come in. Having to ask for help and being able to accept help or being looked after is very new to people who are determined never to be vulnerable. And in the new we can often find the seeds of potential for change in attitude.

Crises tend to happen at times when we feel brittle or rigid inside, when we are unable to be flexible or dance to the rush of demand upon us. Many people who have attained maturity and wisdom tend not to have crises as such but will speak of times of extremes where they are called upon to practise bare attention.

Testing out

Some people speak of their 'trials by fire'; of their 'passage on the long sea journey'; of their being 'brought to their knees'. Part of the journey of initiation is that we are tested and this testing forges a strong mettle within us. We come through this process able to discriminate, endure, remain present with whatever is asked of us and just get on with it. We may feel tested again and again, until we scream out 'not this *again!*' Sometimes, it is when we have lost sight of ourselves and the path we are on, when all is given up, and we feel forsaken by all, and by all that has had meaning for us, that the dawn begins to break and a new awareness begins to assert itself. In this process the rough, redundant, inappropriate coatings are burned or washed off. The base substances of the ego personality are stressed and stretched, placed in the great cauldron or the vast alchemical flask for the forging process of change to take place.

There are many examples of this in our ancient myths and religious texts. There is the testing through temptation of Christ in the wilderness. The temptations of Mara appearing to the Buddha towards the end of his journey to enlightenment. In *The Magic Flute*, the lovers Papageno and Pamina have to undergo the tests and trials of silence, blindfolding, mistaken identity to prove their commitment to love. Jungian psychology interprets the story of Eros and Psyche, described by Apuleius in *The Golden Ass*, as an allegorical story of the awakening, discriminating and coming together in divine marriage of masculine and feminine energies. Psyche has dared to look at Eros while he was sleeping and been overwhelmed by his beauty. Before she can become reunited consciously with Eros, she has to make a voyage where she is tested as to her focus, discrimination and discipline. In the underworld, she has to gather wool from wild sheep with poisonous horns in a dangerous valley, but she is assisted by a green reed. When she has to sort out the mixed seeds of lentils, beans, poppy seed and millet by morning an army of ants helps her all night. Having come through these tests, only then can she be in a mature and equal relationship with Psyche. *Eros*

We may dream of having to climb a mountain, pass through a narrow gully or over a rope bridge, make our way across the ocean or a swirling river, cross a border without a map or passport, wander anxiously through a maze or labyrinth.

If we experience our testings as fire, our images may well be of burning. If our images are watery we will feel awash with feeling or as if we could weep forever. We might be caught in imagery connected to the earth such as feeling entombed, trapped, held in a womb-like cave with all the lights shut down. One way to experience this testing is to work with the imagery to feel your way literally with the quality and specific aspect of the image as your guide of feeling, thinking, sensing and intuition. If we give each of these functions a corresponding image of water, air, earth and fire, we can perhaps feel what function we are being most tested on. For example, if we feel we are in a dark cave with all the lights out, we will have to move about very carefully probably on our hands and knees and go about tapping walls, smelling things and listening hard for the subtlest of sounds. If we are used to seeing clearly, having the lights on in our life and seeing where were are going, this test will be for us to develop other ways of seeing and hearing. If we feel we are in a deep river or tossed about at sea when we are used to having our feet on firm ground, we will have to learn to become swimmers and pearl divers. If we feel we have been thrown up in the air like a bird without wings we will have to learn about safe flight – perhaps about expressing our thoughts and ideas in a clearer, airy way.

Some images of initiation are of being blindfolded so that we cannot see in the old way. Our usual methods of communication are blocked so that others have to grow. This is the test. The testing makes us ask what is being asked of us? And, what does this serve?, rather than trying to rectify things back to how they were. The test has no examiners but ourselves and passing through the levels of testing automatically seems to bring us into new levels of awareness. If we fail to acknowledge the test and to move into open questioning, we can get very stuck. It is then that our fears increase and our need for literalization to provide concrete answers gets in the way of our asking and listening. Our images begin to fade and our imagination dries up, its energy fuelling obsession with control and change at any cost. If we fasten our feelings onto what has not happened for us, on our unlived life, or on our disappointments with other people who have let us down we will remain in a psychological limbo. And it can be tempting. Easier in one way to blame miseries or incapacities on what has not happened, than to brave it through to something not yet known. And we desperately need the inspiration of the structures as laid down in ancient rites and stories to guide us. So that we can fully claim the hero or heroine within us and all the energy needed for the work. In *The Hero with a Thousand Faces*, Joseph Campbell writes:

> The psychological dangers through which earlier generations were guided by the symbols and spiritual exercises of their mythological and religious inheritance, we today (in so far as we are unbelievers, or, if believers, in so far as our own inherited beliefs fail to represent the real problems of contemporary life) must face alone, or at best, with only tentative, impromptu, and not very effective guidance. This is our problem as modern, 'enlightened' individuals, for whom all gods and devils have been rationalised out of existence.[3]

Part of initiation is to be tested by means of having things stolen from us, ripped away by the tricksterish Mercury, or coming off a pedestal, falling from a great height, and we may find that we are highly accident prone. The overall effect of all the means of testing is that we are being humbled, and our old survival ways of coping are being removed. We have to visit the shadowlands of our psyche and feel its darkness and indifferentiated state. This means being filled with rage or envy, feeling constantly anxious or having panic attacks, feeling fixated on someone else, jealous. Whatever has been in the shadow of our being has invited us to really feel its true quality. We may feel we will be drowned or buried alive within it. It really does feel like a trial by fire.

The triumph of initiation is that we move into receiving all that our life brings as if it were a gift. We do not hold on to old structures which are being made redundant, nor do we make structures and excuses out of a mythological or psychological understanding, for it is possible to use the naming of the process as an excuse to escape from actual risk of engagement. People who say 'that was my shadow' or 'I've worked through my feminine, my father/mother complex', or who lean on some abstract or theoretical structure as an explanation for their behaviour may well be missing the point of the actual surrender needed for initiation to show us its most golden aspects. The hardest test perhaps is that we actually do not know where we are going or what this travelling will bring us into, and we need to

---

[3]   Campbell, J., *The Hero with a Thousand Faces*, Bollingen Series (1999).

stay with this not knowing as a vital part of our commitment. Later will the shape and words appropriate be able to be born.

The dark night of the soul

The night sea journey and the dark night of the soul are graphic images for the long protracted experience of the initiation process. In the chapter on waiting (Chapter 14), we look at many of the questions and issues that come alive when nothing seems to be shifting or changing in our internal or external life. We have to undergo periods of seclusion, isolation or the monotony of long repetitive hard graft. The metaphor of the dark night can help us to conceptualize where we are, and to join in with those heroes and heroines who have travelled this journey and survived to become wise commentators as we have encountered so far in this book, such as Jung, Dante, Goethe, Picasso. Picasso's dark night of the soul came in his early twenties after his closest friend committed suicide. Then he entered his 'blue period' of melancholy and depression, mourning for his friend and the loss of life. He painted sad pierrots and harlequins, those mythical and carnival figures who carry so much of the language and pathos of being between two worlds, and, towards the end of this seven-year stage, he began to paint the mother and child images, as perhaps his psyche was emerging with the birth of a new life.

Masculine and feminine

Part of our journey of initiation psychologically is to move into a different relationship with masculine and feminine energies. We looked, in Chapter 1, at how these two opposites often become polarized within us, or we get lopsided. Feminine consciousness can be seen as our relationship with the principles of life itself, with figures that carry the energy of the goddess. This means being at home with instinctuality and with the acceptance of good and bad. The goddess carries two faces which are two sides of the same. Out of her womb, comes life and we return into her earth womb after death. She can be mother earth, fecund, creative, nurturing, loving, and she can be the stagnating mother who binds her new life to her for her jealous ends, Kali, the terrible destroyer. Figures representing the goddess invite us into a relationship with the here and now, with paradox and ambivalence in order to help us develop an attitude of relationship that can embrace all life. When we enter a relationship with ourselves in a true way this shifts the ways in which we enter relationships with others, the world. When we embrace the reality that we are all connected, we become more committed to 'inter-being'. We only know ourselves through being in relationship, with the intimacy this demands. All mindfulness and meditation practices demand that we enter into the world of our preoccupations, often of a deeply emotional kind, and are in kind relationship with them in order to develop and steady our practice.

When we revisit or remeet the masculine principle, the 'father', we enter our relationship with authority and with masculine consciousness. This is currently being redefined in a post-feminist culture, but from a psychological sense this would seem to be a relationship with discipline. Our initiation is to face the father, his absence, conditions, and the forms he may have taken in our life. Sometimes he appears as an ogre, a stripping-away voice, judging, belittling, putting us down. As we face this and stand up to it, we learn our own masculine-focused voice, we learn what is appropriate discipline so that we may be disciples of our own actions.

When masculine and feminine move together, the feminine principle is the receptive vehicle within which our ideas are fertilized and actualized. The more precise we become, the more we need to be wider, the more we must open.

Initiation rites and rites of passage

Initiation rites are ancient phenomena embedded within every culture, but possibly today much disguised or completely absent in western nations. The traditional rites induce and channel suffering in order to create the threshold between emergent

81

states of being or developing stages of life. The rites offer a ritualized loss of control and organization of chaos. They recognize that these aspects are important ingredients in the process of change and development of the human psyche.

Religious culture carries initiation rites both for those who take holy vows and the steps into initiation as a priest, monk or nun. And for those committed to a religious tradition there are the initiation rites into the body of the church of first communion, confirmation; and, within the Jewish culture, the bar mitzvah, which celebrates both the emergence of the male child into the next phase and into his spiritual awareness and commitment. The process involves following a creed as laid down by scripture and being guided by a person who knows these scriptures well and who has undergone the appropriate initiatory rites.

The timing of initiation rites of passage frequently coincide with major social and physiological changes such as the rites surrounding birth, with the midwives making preparation for the process of labour and to deliver a newborn child. Following birth, there are many customs of welcoming and blessing a new child while 'heaven lies above us in our infancy' as Wordsworth wrote. The pagan ceremony of churching – presenting the new child to mother earth at a crossroad – was developed by the formal western church into the 'churching' of women after childbirth. They were not allowed outside until they and their child had been presented into church and to God, after the forty-day 'quarantine'.

Menstruation rites, now completely disappeared in western culture, celebrate the biological emergence of a girl into woman and link together the body reality of ovulation and fecundity with the spiritual sense of wonder at the potential for procreation. Rather than rejoicing today, most girls greet this occurence with the idea that now they have the 'dreaded curse'. There are also seclusion rites in the Masai for menstruating women who have permission to withdraw and be alone, away from the company of men while they are menstruating.

Circumcision in Masai cultures is undertaken by boys at puberty when they feel ready. It is highly ritualized with several spectators in a public place. The boy stares at his mother throughout – it can take up to five minutes without any kind of anaesthetic – and she screams his agony for him. He must remain silent. After circumcision, the boy becomes a warrior and lives on the edge of the bush with other boys away from the village. A later ritual ceremony within Masai culture is the *Eunoto* annual festival in which warriors graduate to junior elders. They perform the famous high jumping dance for hours. The jumping induces a trance through hyperventilation and is also a ritual time for taking drugs boiled from the roots of tree bark. This process marks a ritual and rite of passage in the life of the warriors, who then go on to acquire wives and cattle. Perhaps our boiled-down equivalent of these socially organized and contained ceremonies takes the form of the acid trances, the rave and crack-sharing among young people looking for a way to lose themselves and emerge different, or as new. But however these 'rites' are attempted, we have limited their naming to the pathologies of addiction where the containment for chaos and loss of control is a detoxification unit or prison cell and where most of the ritualized sharing takes place in grotty basements or in lavatories, or is lost altogether.

Then there are the rites of passage involving withdrawal from the general tribe, being alone and surviving nights in the desert or bush, and the blooding and sharing of secret passwords before entry into the next clan or group.

Dancing and chanting, drumming, fasting, bathing in water and the Dionysian and Bacchanalian rites of drunkenness and sexual orgy all offer the experience of rites of passage when changes in consciousness are required to bring about the movement from one level to another. These are not culs-de-sac but rites organized, established and provided safely by experienced elders as an important container for the often dangerous and lonely process of change.

The importance of ritual

Ritual helps to build a bridge between our internal and external worlds. It offers an external recognition for internal change. Ritual feeds the soul, not the ego. In ritual, we clear a space from

83

the everyday where what we need to have acknowledged is boiled down into its essentials. We clean and sweep in order to create a sacred space. We empty ourselves from the clutter of chatter or thought. We choose to make an offering into the space – our energy, our prayers, our thoughts about someone or an event, a meditation. We light a candle, which represents the life principle. We step into a cleared sacred space and let go of what has been past, or become used up and stand empty. We may experience purification and tranformation. Our ritual may be shared and acknowledged by others as our witnesses. We may express gratitude and be dedicated to the new energy. We may give or receive gifts, new clothes. We may celebrate by singing, dancing, sharing wine. We will have created a circle of love.

In Part Four, we will be revisiting the importance of regular ritual as a practice for the stepping stones for the edge. When we ritualize something, however ordinary, we honour and invest that moment with importance and meaning and we offer the opportunity for soul gathering, for sacred energy to emerge. It is via the ritualization of events that they become sacred, precious. This may be simply the ritual of bathing each day, of meditation, of creating a meal or a fire. Making it into a ritual means that we invest the moment with more thought and energy than when we do things automatically, as if by rote, or as a labouring chore. Creating our own rituals for being on the edge means engaging in the meaning of initiation, making it work for us.

One women described to me the sad aftermath of her husband's death and how she felt she would never pick herself up again to face life on her own.

> I'd got used to lighting a candle in the mornings and putting it on an old chest where I also kept precious books, letters and objects such as stones and shells. Over a year on, a friend said 'are you still in mourning or are you preparing for something?'

> I thought about that and realized that inside I was actually emerging and the light was for myself as well as for him. I was getting ready to embrace life, after my husband's death. So, I had been mourning, but was also preparing, and I had this feeling that each day I was offering something up to the universe, and in turn it was speaking to me.

This woman with her candle, the man with the salt baths, others with their campfires keeping the flame alight to light the way, those with sacred waters who seek the blessing for their crossing. The rituals of prayer, meditation, chanting, singing, sharing silent walks with friends, building with stones like Jung, painting out one's innermost passage like many artists who leave their works for us to share. We do not have to be the 'expert' artist, writer or poet, but let our own unique inner artistry weave its way via the ritualization to bear witness to their engagement with the sacred process going on within.

Death and rebirth

Part of initiation involves the experience of death and rebirth. The death may be an actual death, in the form of something or someone to whom we are attached. It could be the death of a part of ourselves that has outlived its usefulness, or it may be in the form of a living death, the feeling that we are going on biologically living but feel psychologically or emotionally dead. Stanislav Grof, whose pioneering work with the impact of prenatal experience on our consciousness memory and capacity is recorded in his writing and research, says in *The Stormy Search for the Self*:

> the 'dying' and the agony during the struggle for rebirth reflect the actual pain and vital threat of the biological birth process. The ego death that precedes rebirth is the death of our old concepts of who we are and what the world is like, which were forged by the traumatic imprint of birth. As we are purging these old programs by letting them emerge into consciousness they are becoming irrelevant and are, in a sense, dying. As frightening as this process is, it is actually very healing and transforming.[4]

Grof goes on to name the sense of annihilation common to death and rebirth experiences, many of which we have been exploring in the properties of the edge. This could come

---

[4]   Grof, S. and C., *The Stormy Search for the Self*, p. 75, Thornsons (1990).

through a sense of emotional disaster, intellectual and philosophical defeat, ultimate moral failure, even spiritual damnation – as if all reference points for our life are being destroyed. It seems that once we have surrendered to this process as part of our initiatory experience and are prepared to undergo the trauma involved, we are reborn. This is not dissimilar to the surrender of the shaman to the unconscious processes necessary for healing, sometimes wounding and maiming themselves to induce the pain and suffering needed to alter the level of conscious awareness and to enter completely the intimate space of the person suffering.

All these ways, recorded in the ancient rites, the stories, patterns and myths of many different cultures show how rebirth through death is the most potent image for all major experiences. When we accept death as part of life with no divisions we allow something else to come in, we allow the new, the dawn to be heralded.

The process is one of accepting that some aspect within our outer or inner life is dying and needs to be allowed to die. This is often hard for us because we cannot see beyond the immediate death and we fear there will be nothing beyond.

If we look into nature we see many examples of death and rebirth. From the savage pruning we give to rose trees and our other plants, to the burn of autumn as if a last fire before surrender to the dark of winter, and being underground. Then, after several months there is spring and the emergence of astonishing pale green shoots of such freshness and vigour, rising out of the stubborn, frozen earth and in the woods. We wonder at the force and strength of it all. However much our earth has been plundered and pillaged, it still sends up these wonders.

Peak experience and unitive consciousness

The goal of initiation is that we pass through the different stages and emerge into another place that appears to have been waiting for us. This is not to say that this place is 'there' or 'meant' in the concrete sense, or that it is laid down by any decree. Whatever we are able to forge within our experience creates the new. It is a mixture of our response, our capacity and the external forces that we are able to muster in the life in which we find ourselves. This place may not be distinguishable from other geography we have known externally but its feel will be very different. The way this place is experienced by different people varies hugely. Some people actually see a great light, feel a surge of passion or intense feeling of well-being. We may begin to feel truly alive for the first time in years, are aware that our attention span is more intense than ever before. Sometimes there is a sense of radiance within and without that is like a permanent smile. Always there is a feeling of being fresh. One of the invitations from Thich Nhat Hanh when asked to comment upon the return to the everyday world after a retreat is to 'keep yourself fresh'.

Peak experience refers to those moments when we move beyond our everyday awareness and into a state of 'wholeness' or cosmic awareness. People describe these times as being enlightened into something beautiful and whole, where the entire world is seen in its fullness and vivid colours, where every sensation is felt absolutely. Some of these experiences are felt in just moments, or time lasting into hours or days, and after the intense period is over the person moves about the world with his/her consciousness permanently changed. These times are perhaps the nearest we come to an experience of wholeness and of being united with the entire universe.

We may experience a profound sense of the inner marriage – the coming together of masculine and feminine consciousness which leads us into the path of wisdom – when we speak with both masculine and feminine aspects, when we are in balance, in the rhythm of the eternal dance. When people come into a place of alignment within themselves, the warmth and light and sense of groundedness – that sense of being truly present – tends to spread out to others. People with this light – who may have literally 'seen the light' – will tend to shine like a beacon in their attractiveness. For it is something of this light, this knowing, this level of acceptance that we all yearn for. The smile on the beatific face of His Holiness the Dalai Lama tells of this light and so do many of the enigmatic, beatific, lit-up faces that painters such as Michelangelo, Leonardo, Vermeer have given us. It was a face such as this on the nine-year-old Beatrice that initiated Dante onto his great mythic and poetic adventure.

These experiences bring us more fully into the body of man and womankind and into the animate world itself. In this way, our life becomes dedicated to the wider purposes of living and particularly today, to our survival on earth. Then, it is not limited just to our own small individual purposes but offers a way of being that could unite us within all sentient beings and feel our lives dedicated to sharing our energy with others and working toward the relief of suffering.

Awakening and return

After a long journey, particularly one with sharp edges, as we have been exploring, we feel tired, and yet awake. Often we feel childlike because we are approaching our life with the newfound wonder akin to that which we first experience in childhood. We may have had transcendent and numinous experiences which still feel fresh. We feel more than ever the initiate, but the initiate to a much wider sense of ourselves and to life. And our life goes on. The shop on the corner is still the same but it somehow looks different. The friends and foes we are used to grappling with on a Monday morning are still there but we speak to them differently and some of them speak differently to us. It is the same as in the Zen story of the monk looking for enlightenment who travelled far and wide in his search for the master who would teach him. After crossing many mountains and rivers, he finally came to a place where there lived a great and wise master. The monk was given food at the kitchen and waited for his audience. When he had responded to the master's question about his search and his journey, and after decribing the dangers, the animals the dangerous crossings on his way to meet the master, the master asked him: 'you must be tired after a long journey, have you yet eaten?' When the monk replied that, yes, he had, the master said 'then go wash your bowl'.

Before enlightenment we chop wood. After enlightenment we chop wood. Everything has changed inside, and yet nothing has changed. There are still chores to be done, people to attend to, letters to answer and tasks to be planned. But we come to them in a very different way. Life does not get easier, nor does it get nicer, more problem free, but our attitude to our engagement with out own mortal life has changed dramatically. We come through something and we emerge as ourselves, able to listen to our own wise self inside, not needing to be a guru or evangelist, but we speak from our own hearts as and when we find things and as we see things. We may see the world with fresh eyes, with a regained innocence and sense of wonder, a delight and joy, and with our ability to receive the awe-inspiring aspects of creation fresh and marvelling. And, because we have survived the darkest, rockiest, storm-tossed ride, we owe a debt to the mysteries of the dark. In the same way that Persephone ate pomegranate-seeds in the underworld signifying that she must return there for a proportion of every year when winter is upon us, so we must make a promise to let the darkness speak to us as and when it needs and to remain in awe at the revelation of the dark's own mysteries.

Part Two

ASPECTS OF THE EDGE

5

Preparing to Explore the Edge

This next section maps nine aspects of the edge. Each aspect has its own landscape, history, feeling quality, associations with both light and darkness. The maps attempt to chart and describe what it is like to have to surrender to the aspect for a period of time; weeks, months, perhaps years. The maps also attempt to chart a loose guide to being there and offer some thoughts on how we might bear the psychological tension. Each aspect of the edge will be unknown to us when we first come upon it and therefore new and frightening. Until being on the edge has become a place of transition and the threshold to change, it is an alien place where we feel alone and abandoned. There is often a long deep melancholy and monotony interrupted by extremes of feeling and non-feeling, and an ever-present fear of going over the edge into darkness.

Negotiating the edge can be an opportunity – to harness powerful inner energies and to break through to something new, and it can also mean an encounter with pitfalls that result in our falling into our personal chasm. As with all new and difficult experiences, there are potentially positive aspects as well as pitfalls and dangers. How we experience ourselves being on the edge, what it provokes within us, what it invites us to fight or dance among all become part of the journey we make. On a personal level, it is a soul-forging experience the dimension of which we will not see clearly until we are able to get some distance from the edge itself. On a transpersonal level, the edge becomes the place where we soften our attachment to the hard edges of dualistic thinking and remain open to a greater spaciousness that is a requirement of spiritual experience.

The personal and transpersonal forging processes are the crucial element in our whole journey and affect the journey's outcome. If we do not engage with what is happening to us and never move away from our first reaction to the dangerous new, we remain stuck, or hang in limbo; or, we may be swept away by the very forces we are trying to resist.

At the edge, we are also prey to false prophets that would seem to offer relief through their enticements, but who may lead us into the blind alley of illusion, addiction or suicidal impulse. We need guiding principles to allow us to make the wisest judgements and selection and not stumble blindly and passively on unable to read the warning signs. It may be that encounters with false prophets are actually part of the journey we are to make. Our challenge then is to develop discrimination. Like in the fairytale of Vasilisa, we have to learn to separate poppy seeds from grain. It may be that a period of feeling stuck or in limbo or being in the blind alley of addiction holds within it the very enlightening experience that awakens us to the seriousness of our predicament. The aim of a map or chart is to help us see the kind of landscape we are likely to encounter and make the necessary preparation. Sometimes the map does not become really alive for us until after we have visited the place. Then it serves as a powerful record of the extent of our travels that we revisit on each reading.

Having examined aspects of the edge, we may choose to stay there, recognizing them as the places we live best. But our choice then is an informed and conscious one rather than an avoidant or lazy refuge.

And for people whose lives are defined by the edge because of their extreme personal encounters with hardship, mindless violence, badness or long-term painful physical or mental abuse and illness, the greatest triumph may be surviving to live on the edge of their bleak universe and not letting it destroy them.

Each of the nine aspects of the edge contain both the potential for breaking through and for breaking down. True break-through always involves the process of breaking up to breakdown in order to break through. We have to allow a death in order to make way for a birth. Breaking through is going on at the same time as breaking down. For James Hillman: 'The death motif is always present at the beginning of change and appears in order to make way for transformation. The creative force kills as it produces the new. The flower withers around the swelling pod. The snake sheds its skin' (*Suicide and the Soul*).

Break-up is usually experienced most painfully by the ego personality where it hurts the most. Identifying the aspect that is most engaged with the suffering of break-up means naming what it is we feel we are losing. It could be a sense of being in control for example. So our question needs to be, control of what? If we feel our identity under attack, we need to be asking with what or whom have we identified ourselves.

Overall questions when exploring the maps of the edge are:

1 What is it within me that most needs to undergo change?
2 Which aspect of myself has perhaps been overvalued and which undervalued?
3 What part of me, my behaviour or my attachments are most at stake right now?

It may be the least-known part of us which suffers. In break-up and breakdown we always find ourselves in a situation where nothing that has gone before helps us to cope. We are in the midst of something completely new and therefore alien, we are unpractised and this is what makes us feel lost.

PREPARATION FOR EXPLORATION OF THE EDGE

A healing attitude

Recent consciousness research at Oxford has found that we can send healing, and transmit love to be received by another person with whom we have a connection, even though walls, countries and death itself are present. We can have this capacity, which allows for the idea that nothing is ever lost, that our attention may be placed and serve a recipient, all of our life. Every one of us can do this for ourselves and for others whom we know are suffering.

Awakening to a hunger on the personal, soulful level brings us more deeply in touch with our innermost self and the basis on which we have lived our lives so far. When we decide to become committed to serve our soulful needs both individually and around us in the outside world, we are ready to move along the edge. We then take up the patterns of a spiritual path that becomes our thread. Our light and our guide. It is there for us to return to at every turn in the narrow way. It is there at the narrowest of places where nothing much is to be seen. It is there when there seems nothing but darkness and despair.

Maitri

Any journey we take which involves listening to ourselves and exploring our minds needs to be done in a spirit of loving kindness. Maitri means both loving kindness and unconditional friendliness to oneself. Many of us are dominated by quite critical and judgemental thinking, especially when things do not go well. We blame ourselves or others. We allow harsh voices to enter into our inner landscape.

'Why don't you?'; 'You should ... '; 'Oh, you're just hopeless'. Often these aggressive voices inside ourselves lead to our giving up simply being present with our experience. We hear them too much or we become overwhelmed by their hostility. We need a different attitude when we begin to explore ourselves deeply. We need to develop a note of maitri and to hear all our voices with this kindness to ourselves. This will allow us to step a little further to the heart of ourselves and not be dogged by persistent negativity and aggression.

The wise, compassionate observer

Because the edge is often so very narrow and cramped, or awash with confusion, we need to develop an observing self that is able to stand aside, compassionately, and bear witness to the detail of our process. This means developing an 'I' that sees 'me' in whatever forms it finds 'me'. It means that this 'I' needs to be full of maitri and compassion and be the kind, observing witness. This is not a detached position or a cynical watcher. It is a part of us that grows in wisdom as it stands in this vital observing role. The wise, compassionate observer will always be our friend – it may not reflect things we like – but it will be objectively discriminating and truthful in order for us to be freed from the pitfalls of delusion. Much suffering is created out of our delusions about who we are and what other people expect from us. Many of our sufferings are created by our projections onto ideas, people or events, which give us an illusion of good things, things we believe we need to make us happy. The wise observer sees this and is compassionate to our craving and longing at the same time as nudging our awareness in order that we might discriminate.

Embracing fear

The edge is always fearful. Fear often leads us to avoid, prevaricate or refuse the call to life and to be awake. Know that you will be afraid. See if you can make a relationship with your fear. Fear is normal. In early life, it is protective in its instinctual sense, but natural and appropriate fear (like of a tiger coming up behind from which we need the adrenalin rush from fear to send blood to our legs to run) easily becomes overlaid with learned fears. Fear of what others will think, of punishment, being unloved, left behind, lost. Our biological fear is then overlaid with mental learning and attitude. We even learn to be fearful of fear itself, not wanting to feel, becoming numb instead until fear propels us into some incident, or floods out as in a full-blown panic attack.

Fear can be seen as one of the fierce gatekeepers of the edge, one which will test us even before we have approached.

Notice your fear and its nature. Explore it a little. Be kind to it, speak to it with loving kindness. Allow it to reveal itself to you in all forms. Is it the child in you that is afraid? Is it the unknown of which you are afraid and wonder if you can cope or survive what is new, even alien?

What would you do if you had a frightened person sitting next to you on your sofa? Would you tell them to pull themselves together or would you put your arm around them and let the smell and trembling of their fear be absorbed into your coat? Can you be alongside your fear in the same way? Know it, get really close to it, embrace it however ugly you find it, put your hand in its and move forward with it.

Self-awareness and self-pity

The main goal shared by most psychotherapies is that a person become self-aware. This means knowing ourselves just as we are, with all our personal history, our wounds, likes and dislikes, our struggles, traits, no-go areas, our shadow, our strengths, joys. When we are self-aware, we know the places that are going to be the most demanding, or challenge or hurt the most. We can anticipate them, even be thrown by them, caught off guard, but soon we are able to recognize something of what this has been about. When we are not self-aware we tend to project everything onto other people, places or events. We blame others for what goes wrong, we indulge in self-pity.

Self-pity is when we are unable to be truly present with our suffering, just as it is. We attach some thought to our feeling such as 'I'm always going to feel like this and will never be happy again', or 'no one knows what it's really like', or 'nothing else is as bad as this', or 'if my mum and dad had allowed me a bike I would be more independent'. The moment we step into this space we lose sight and touch with our real feelings and abandon them. We step into a whole dialogue involving past and future possible events and a whole history of what might or might not happen. Of course we are trying not to suffer. We are trying to divert ourselves from our pain. And we all do it and will continue to do it. The art of becoming self-aware is that we catch ourselves doing it. We say, kindly, with maitri – 'Ah – here you are, going on a diversion again. Let's stop this thought pattern now and return to what you were feeling. What does that feeling most need from you? How can you just stay with it as it is?'

Personal talisman

The dark places are all best visited by taking a thread or light to help befriend the way. You may wish to imagine your own talisman for the following journey of properties of the edge. Something that is for you personal, special, and sacred. Take some time over finding an image for this with your eyes closed. Some people know immediately what special object they would wish to take as talisman. They may already have imbued some object with special meaning, something which has seen them through in previous difficult times. A stone or shell, crystal, bible, *mala*, beads, photograph, animal, inner guide. A talisman is different from a lucky charm. It is the image which carries the energy of our inner wise knowing self, or transpersonal self. Sometimes what becomes a talisman is an object or image our ego personality would not choose for aesthetic or sentimental reasons. Knowing this frees you to take the authentic energy from this place and what has been chosen for you.

Imagining a safe place

Always begin any kind of inner exploration from a place of safety and return to this place after you have ventured into difficult or alien territory. This is very important when responding to the powerful images that occur when we are on the edge. Always keep an image of a safe place, and always remember to touch base with your talisman.

A safe place can be any place we know or one we find within our imaginary space. If it is hard to imagine such a place, keep coming back to the idea of safety, a safe space all of your own, while you are going about your everyday world. Let the image appear to you in its own time. Images for safe places have included a garden, field, river, tree, bush, room, cave or armchair that offer sanctuary. Safe places may also change as we move to different aspects of the edge. If your safe place begins to change, fasten your eye onto one quality of the safety within this place and let this be your guide.

Sometimes our only safe spot is in the form of a stepping stone amid a rush of water or moving ground. Grip the stone firmly with your feet or hands. If it begins to feel as if it is ready to start shifting, look around for the next safe stepping stone to be your crouching or standing place. Treat the process just like a series of stepping stones, quietly step off the one you have found and begin to find another, and know that this is your anchor for the moment.

You may like to spend some time either holding an object of your choice, or imagining a special place which offers you sanctuary, a place you may go back to as and when you need.

Spiritual practice

Leading a spiritually aware life begins with our own everyday practice of remaining truly present with every moment. As we wash dishes, we know that we are washing dishes. As we walk to the bus, we know that we are walking to the bus. As we speak with another, we remain present with the act of speaking and of listening. And these daily rituals of remaining mindful of the true nature of every moment are nourished by meditation practice. Each day try sitting with your breath for around twenty minutes at first. Simply breathing in and then out, noting a long breath or a short breath. When distractions occur in the form of thoughts, just note them and return to the breath. The Zen Buddhist master Thich Nhat Hanh has this breath poem:

> I have arrived
> I am home.
> In the here
> In the now
> I am solid
> I am free
> In the ultimate, I dwell.

During the moments of meditation practice there is stillness.

There is no need to run any more. This small practice of sitting with the breath each day and returning to the breath when we feel we have lost our way will be an important friend. Always there is the potential for touching the peace and beauty of an eternal stillness.

Everything we do, think and say matters. It affects our outside world and the people in it and it certainly affects our inside living. The physical act of smiling has been proved to stimulate more endorphins in the brain. Leading a spiritually aware life does not mean renouncing matter and begging on the street. What it means is making a commitment to the true nature of each moment in which we have a relationship with the here and now. It is this relationship that develops our awareness of the impact and consequences of all our actions. The teacher who teaches from the heart, the policeman who exercises wise counsel, the shopkeeper who looks her customer in the eye, the doctor and nurse who are mindfully present with their patients' pain all serve the wider flow of spiritual energy. This makes a qualitative difference to our world.

6

Chaos

The Centre that I cannot find
Is known to my unconscious mind;
I have no reason to despair
Because I am already there.

My problem is how not to will;
They move most quickly who stand still:
I'm only lost until I see
I'm lost because I want to be.

W. H. Auden, from 'The Maze', *Collected Poems* (1940)

Part of being on the edge involves a return to the chaos of our once undifferentiated state of being, but with both the curse and joy of consciousness. Our eyes are open now, but it feels as if our ego is under assault and no longer feeling in charge. A brush with inner chaos is always frightening at first. We have no accepted maps for this experience. Chaos is experienced both inside and outside. Our internal chaos may be triggered by outside chaotic events; or, we may create chaos externally because of the chaos of our internal milieu. What is chaos for one person will be different for another.

When we feel on the edge, where there is not much space, any kind of chaos can seem more alarming than usual. External chaos can often be worked through by organization and planning, by negotiation, stepping back, waiting for the decks to clear. But when chaos seems to have crept inside us, dealing with both inside and outside can feel overwhelming. And on the edge we do not know where we are going, which in itself can feel chaotic. If we are experiencing swings of mood, feeling tearful and overwhelmed one minute, angry and hostile another, this can feel chaotic. We just don't know where we are.

Chaos can be everything we know undone and scattered, our sense of order in turmoil or violated. We may feel we are spinning and falling, disintegrating, fragmenting, our everyday 'I' in eclipse. Chaos can be created by the regressive pull to return to a state of unconsciousness, to feeling infantile, childlike and helpless.

We may view our choices as being only the polarized 'give in and let it take over' or 'shut it out and fight it to the death'. A third position of choice could be to follow the call to recognize we are dealing with chaos, name the substance of our chaos as best we can and thus invest our experience with the authority of a scientific approach. One way to meet chaos is to meet the images chaos brings.

What is our individual image and relationship with that image of chaos? Images of the unborn, of being *in utero*, in the pressure and chaotic world of the birth process, having no voice, no words, being sucked into a whirlpool or held in a vice may dominate our dreams and waking moments.

We may experience chaos in waves or floods, in moments, or it may come and go unexpectedly.

On a mundane level, many people who live ordered lives during the week, structured with work appointments and deadlines, experience the unstructured weekend space as chaotic and seek to fill it with order or dull the anxiety chaos brings with alcohol or busyness. And the opposite occurs. A contemplative person used to enjoying a quiet life of solitude will experience noise, movement, travel, deadlines, people, busyness, cities, as having a chaotic dimension. We tend to fear chaos until we can control it, giving it a firm edge or boundary so that it cannot take us over.

PRIMORDIAL IMAGES

Chaos is a universal fear, promoting in humans the desire for civilization and control and initiating the building of firm structures and buildings, and the creation of containing bodies such as the church, family and government, and national defences like army, navy and missile bases. Thick bush and brambles can be conquered by structuring roads and creating prairie fields. For nature appears chaotic and left alone will both devour as well as nurture. The primeval forest, the ocean depths, the desert wastelands are all primordial images that often present as our image of chaos. Within these images are both the swirling dark depths in which we may become lost, and also the seeds of systems of order that link us to patterns and rhythms of nature way beyond our wildest civilized dreams.

SHADOW SEEN AS CHAOS

When people or things viewed and feared as chaotic are repressed in consciousness and held back they fall into the shadow areas of unconscious life, both in our individual lives and within our collective groups. Gypsies and travellers, the circus people, tramps and the homeless and nomadic people are feared for their non-conforming attitudes, and their wild, untamed energy is viewed as antisocial. The long rule of apartheid can be seen as an attempt by one group (a white minority) to control another (a majority group of blacks). The unconscious motive behind this was perhaps to keep back an energy force not understood, but judged and feared as chaotic, which might harm the everyday orderly rule of the perceived controlled life. In our own individual psyches, images of the tramp, wastrel, gypsy may come to haunt us during times of chaos, especially if we have repressed the more chaotic energies of instinctual life. Conscious fears of ending life as the tramp under the river embankment arch or the bag lady shuffling in slippers laden with plastic bag parcels often appear when we are overattached to trying to keep the edges of our civilized lives intact. Sometimes our own inner repressed energies come to us in the form of demons and devils, at night in dreams, or by day in the form of other people or causes and situations which carry the force of our projected repressed energy.

Images of chaos may include fighting in the streets, being drunk, a profusion of papers in disorder, bureaucracy taking over life, madness and bedlam, the swirling cesspit, the whirlpool, the untrammelled jungle, sailor lost at sea, the feral creatures who run wild, the prostitute, the snake pit, the haunting demon.

For Joseph Campbell: 'demons are our own limitations. Devil is a god who has not been recognized – the power in us to which we have not given expression and we push it back. Like all repressed energy it builds up and becomes dangerous to the position we are trying to hold'.

For many civilized people, the repression of sexual and instinctual energy for the sake of 'civilized order' and moral superiority causes a wound to the basic natural instinctual nature from which our life force or libido stem and our creativity merges spontaneously. Once held back for fear of its primal chaotic nature, repressed instinctual energy may return to be claimed within us, thus pushing us to the edge of our conforming side. Jung writes that the repressed returns with knife in hand. Energies we have repressed return to claim their rights with a force that is undeniable.

FEAR OF CHAOS

The fear of chaos alone can lead to people clinging on to the edge, to remaining firmly rooted in an outdated mode or constant state of fear. The fear is of descending back into a primal, primitive unconscious state, to become 'like animals', and be at the mercy of a savage untamed energy with no morality or conscious awareness. And yet if we have not been able to feel this energy consciously and know it, we cannot hold a good position with it, it remains cut off out of fear, rather than wrestled with out of respect and awe for something so mighty. And for people cut off from the potential energy of this vital force, life can feel dry, overcontrolled, unexpressive, dull, depressing, and they may take on the symptoms that animals display when captured.

The chaos most feared while on the edge is of going over the edge into breakdown. Fear of breakdown is part of being conscious, but we are more fearful if we have relied upon ego energy alone to get us through. No one would choose breakdown consciously and no one would wish it on anyone else. And yet it is one overwhelming experience which, when met, and then chosen, because it has chosen us, moves us into an extraordinary deep understanding. In *Breakdown*, Margaret writes:

> One part of me was like a tidal wave, a disaster, and I knew it couldn't hold out. Another part of me, a voice somewhere within me would occasionally come up with a clear message, 'suffering is privilege'. I could see that the words made sense but then something in me said 'this is nonsense' and the tidal wave would come back. It is as though there was a seed of light, or hope or strength trying to form itself.

In Part Four we look at suffering more deeply.

REGRESSION

We feel as if something is pulling us back, to the place where our desire for regression is met. Returning to the womb may feel terrifying until we become able to befriend the small life trying to emerge and become aware of the nature of our rebirth. Feeling like a child, primitive, small, infantile and helpless, with all the pains of judgement of childhood experience that we also carry within us, puts us very much on the edge. We feel so little, and want to feel little and yet there is also the adult that judges us from inside, trying to stop us from feeling little. And we revisit our childhood experience and feel again put down, humiliated for our childlikeness, told to grow up, get on with it, stop showing off, stop wanting attention.

Feeling like this and having an adult body is hard. Much is expected of us and often without the permissions of recognizable 'illness' this is hard to accomplish. Many people whose experience of breakdown leads them to psychiatric care speak of giving up in horror and disbelief, at being in a place most feared, and then becoming like children again, with nothing expected and no responsibility within the ward. In *Breakdown* Nadia writes:

> I loved being in hospital. People think you are so mad when you like being in a psychiatric ward. In the ward there was a great deal of love with no expectations, no reservations, no judgements. I found that extraordinary. The people there meant more to me at that time than my husband and that's amazing for I've never loved anyone as much as him. But I really loved some of them. We were like children in many ways, we all had something in common and there was a tremendous amount of support even from the most violent, aggressive people. I found it quite comforting to see people who were behaving quite wildly helping others when they were upset.

Van Gogh described the chaos of his plunges into melancholic despair as 'sometimes moods of indescribable anguish, some-times moments when the veil of time and the totality of circumstances seem torn apart from an instant'. He produced huge amounts of work within the containment of hospital expressing a liking for the order imposed. 'When I have to follow a rule, as here in hospital, I feel at peace'.

The paintings of the St Rémy period are more turbulent than those from Arles. Lubin writes in his biography 'Many are characterized by a linear style that conveys an impression of agitated movement, impulsively executed, yet with demonic control. When he recovered from the long attack of July and August he turned to self portraits. Whilst claiming to have done so for lack of other models, he was probably trying to reconstitute himself after his disorganizing experiences'.[1]

PRIMA MATERIA

Chaos is also the *prima materia*, the original chaotic mass of substance that comes before the Logos principle creates and names the substance of the world we know today, composed of air, earth, fire and water. Early philosophical thinking about the

---

[1] Lubin, A. J., *Stranger on the Earth: A Psychological Biography of Vincent Van Gogh*, Holt, Reinhart & Winston (1972).

prima materia was that this original substance is in potential only, without form, until the process of differentiation into elements is undertaken. The *prima materia* thus form an archetype for all created form and for the psychological life of humans. It is out of the chaotic undifferentiated matter of *prima materia* that form emerges via the process of separation or differentiation, naming and imagining.

In *Anatomy of the Psyche*, Edward Edinger writes:

> Upon the *prima materia* was imposed, as it were, a fourfold structure, a cross, representing the four elements, two sets of contraries, earth and air, fire and water. Psychologically this image corresponds to the creation of the ego out of the undifferentiated unconscious by the process of discriminating the four functions: thinking, feeling, intuition and sensation.[2]

The process of change within the psyche of humans can involve a return to an undifferentiated state while the previously dominant function is in eclipse, in order that the next unfoldment of function may emerge. Or, the return to an undifferentiated state may be a natural response to a traumatic encounter, with death or loss for example, with violence and horror. The process of grieving can often feel like chaos. Order is abolished and rivers of grief run wild and untamed. Any form of psychological suffering can have its periods of chaos, when it feels as if the centre cannot hold and we are rendered down, into a regressive state, feeling helpless and without form. From this undifferentiated childlike state, we are free of ego structure and stricture. The contents of unconscious material and images are able to flow freely through us. Given a safe place and loose structure for care, a person can undergo inner chaos and emerge changed and well.

PSYCHOSIS AND SPIRITUL EMERGENCY

The most severe inner chaos is referred to in medical diagnosis as psychosis. This is a state where an individual loses touch with reality and seems lost in the unconscious world of strange voices and images often ordering him or her about in a fearful and

---

[2]   Edinger., E., *Anatomy of the Psyche*, Open Court (1985).

unrelated way. Since time immemorial men and women have suffered these afflictions and needed to be cared for by family and society. In recent years, what we now call mental health services have attempted to categorize such afflictions in order to decide what best to offer. At present there is no distinction in traditional psychiatric diagnosis between the mystical experience of a spiritual emergency (referred to in Stan Grof's work), creative illness, metanoiac journeys, visionary states, breaking down to breakthrough, and psychotic illness. It seems that all mystical, unusual, non-rational growth experiences take us into the unknown, and may also include experiences which would be diagnosed in medical terms as psychotic. There are many instances where these severe psychotic experiences are short-lived and there is a positive outcome. What seems to make a difference is the view held by the person witnessing the other's journey. If a transpersonal potential is held for the person going through the crisis period of the edge, and a self-organizing process is going on, even when it is not obvious, this can make a tremendous difference in terms of outcome.

The studies initiated by John Weir Perry in the 1950s show that in this place are manifest the seeds of the original self showing a self-organizing principle that knows what it is going on. Drawings from psychotic patients allowed to be free of medication show the use of the circle or mandala symbolism. John Weir Perry's work stemmed from the time a patient suffering psychosis referred to feeling at the centre of her world. She painted a series of images and commented upon them, telling of the process of death and rebirth, the reconciling of opposites through new images and the creation of a new cultural ideology concerned with the nature of governance. The process shifted from concerns of power and prestige to ones of lovingness and social harmony. Alongside this reporting through the paintings was her gradual recovery in terms of restored ego consciousness and the restoration of inner order and outer relatedness. Perry's conclusion from this and other long-term studies of people undergoing psychotic experiences is that there is within each psyche an organizing process going on whose role is a self-healing one and which brings about the restoration of an integrated whole.

CIRCLES AND MANDALAS

The image of the circle, called mandala when it is associated with the sacred, remains the primal symbol operating at the centre of all processes in change. Out of the circle emerges the cross, making the fourfold division, or division of two pairs of opposites. In alchemy, the steps are in four divisions designated by four colours: black, white, red and yellow or gold resulting in the philosopher's stone which reunites the four elements. The circulating-wheel image then is a powerful symbol for the process of change and transformation. The wheel needs to be kept turning in relation to the rule of all of creation, the times of spring, summer, autumn and winter. All need to have their allotted time and space and be in relationship each to the other, and in relation to the times when one is in ascendancy before turning and giving way to the next. And so it is with psychic development, the integration of the four functions of thinking, feelings, intuition and sensation requires the wheel to be turned as each are to be developed.

CHAOS AND CREATIVITY

The nest of creativity is darkness, chaos and confusion. A nest where we are pushed to the edge as the limit of our awareness and our capacity. Where we meet with our gods. Creative work is often the result of this encounter, when out of the nest comes a birth of something new – a new awareness, thought, image, style, revolutionary awakening, philosophical under-standing. The nest, like the alchemist's flask used as a womb for the transformation of base matter – that which has gone before and is now redundant – into something golden in its newness.

As we have seen, the *prima materia* is necessary for the reclaiming and redefining of aspects of ourselves. While in the experience of chaos we will not know what these are or what they are for. Because the experience demands our acceptance and ultimately our receiving the chaos into our reality we have to surrender ourselves consciously to it in order to be in the place

110

where transformation may take place. In this way we are bringing in a scientific approach to what feels very unscientific. Receiving and allowing do not mean that we collapse ourselves into chaos for to do so is to court danger. We need guides and helpers, especially when chaos threatens to take over and the centre within us is in danger of not holding the wheel as it turns within the furnace of the process. Given that we do not know what we are doing or where we are going, which is the work of the ego, we are surrendering ego awareness and consciousness so that another understanding may come our way. We are helped in this by allowing the 'thumbprint of the map-maker' to be on our map. It is unseen, unknown, and even, often, seems to have deserted us. But its trace is in those who have been this way before us, the sages, prophets, masters who, through their teachings, inspire us to keep practising, to let our individual experience and our attention to it, form the guide along our way. We allow these teachings to make this way clearer to us when we are ready to hear it.

When the chaotic, wild self has been directed to be tamed by having to be 'proper', we are denied the energy of the life force. 'Too much domestication breeds out strong and basic impulses to play, relate, cope, rove and commune' (Clarissa Pinkola Estes). Women who run with the wolves. Artists often put themselves on the edge by being the outsider, the recluse, the starving artist in the garret. And internally choosing deprivation, fasting, self-abuse (drink, drugs, poisonous fumes from paint) to develop a cutting edge for their work. Any creative act involves a period of chaos and the building up to concert pitch in order to bring something together out of the chaos; creative acts always involve non-ordinary states of consciousness.

Artists may court chaos for the purpose of getting back into an undifferentiated state. While chaos can instil immediate feelings of fear and revulsion except those who revel and court it for the purpose of creativity, learning to recognize the *prima materia* can take on a different flavour. People have said of the edge, 'it goes on so long. It is grey and tedious. No one knows what it's like to suffer so, there is nothing to show for it'. This is the stuff of *prima materia*. The grit, the ordinary, the unremarkable, the lead chosen by Shakespeare's Portia from Bassanio after the suitors choosing the silver and gold had been rejected: 'you see me Lord Bassanio as I am'.

Recently while undergoing the chaotic aftermath to a serious illness, I sat down one morning to meditate, thinking spontaneously and angrily 'if only I could feel well'. And some voice inside me said 'and what would you do with your wellness?' I knew that at this stage I would have taken my wellness and got back into the fast lane with it, as if that were my right and the ego self would have been in charge once again, with its illusion of control, and that I was not ready, I had not stayed long enough in the process of undifferentiation. Later, when wellness was restored after the long process of chaos, I had come to respect it and use it with much greater awareness.

DANGERS OF CHAOS

Danger comes to our potential whole if we suffer a collapse of the centre because of inundation of unconscious ideas and images. If there is a sense of greater chaos encroaching, containment of an appropriate kind should be sought. Medication can help to hold enough of sense of reality to keep the process of recording the images and ideas moving. Long experiences of feeling chaotic are exhausting and should only be tolerated under wise supervision and when there are vehicles for anchoring the path of the self through writing, storytelling, drawing, sculpting, dancing. Chaos should only be ventured into with appropriate scientific attitude, with the belief in gestation of process of chaos into birth of new order, new life.

EXERCISE: PATHS THROUGH CHAOS

1 Find stepping stones however small for the swirling sea of chaos. Stay on them until they feel as if they are in movement. Then gradually move to the next stepping stone.
2 Name the experience of chaos: paint, sculpt, dance, sing, yell, shout, write, anchor what you experience in one of these

forms, alone or shared with wise witnesses. Dignify your process by giving it form as you go along.

3 If chaos threatens to become unbearable, do not remain alone in it. Recruit helpers. Wise persons. Trusted clinicians. Find friends. If you need more than a wise midwife to your process take the help you need. Medication, safe holding, good containment.

4 While recognizing chaos, dance within it, become the dervish, take up the primordial energy and run with the wildness, move with the whirlwinds and swim with the rivers and floods, burn with the heat of fire and let your passion rise with the temperature. Fly and float and spin and do all this consciously while grounding yourself in the reality of your everyday and the firmness of your stepping stone. Make the experience of chaos as full as you can possibly bear, make it your reality while you are in or near it. Trust its wildness to answer your bravery. Trust your honest heart to find the answers that its call needs.

7

Exhaustion: When the Well Runs Dry

I'm tired
From inside out
my spirit craves for
crumbs of comfort anywhere.
A body lost at sea
I sink in hopeless search
for your attention.
I'm almost proud of my exhaustion
I wear it like a medal
to prove 'she tried'.
But now's the time
to say 'I quit'
and let the pain begin.
Fatigue and pain must fade away
through ticking minutes of my alarm
and only then will I become
more than I was before.

Anon, from *Breakdown*, Elizabeth Wilde McCormick
(1988 and 1997)

Collapsed into the void a man crawls in circles, his paper eyelids closed over dry red sockets. He does not know his hands and knees are bleeding.

A state of wellness can be defined as a healthy productive tension which creates movement and produces activity which is kept in momentum by the balance of effort and rest. Exhaustion is the resulting state created when we continually push ourselves beyond ordinary tiredness and fatigue. Exhaustion is maintained and exacerbated when, instead of stopping to appraise our general situation, we press on disregarding all the physical and psychological signs and rely on will-power alone to keep us going. Alongside this is the fantasy that by our doing so we will close the gap between what is actually happening and what we wish to happen. Exhaustion is a chronically endured feeling of depletion, weariness, anxiety, boredom, emptiness and general malaise bordering on catabolic imbalance. We may talk about feeling dried out, used up, burnt out, as there is no more juice left, and yet we feel compelled, or doomed to carry on.

We become exhausted when external or internal demands stretch our known responses to the absolute limit. This state may carry on for years, and our world may become smaller and smaller as we seek to try to cope.

On the edge we tend to be unaware of the depth of our own fatigue and exhaustion levels. All our attention is focused upon surviving in this narrow place and we tend to use methods we know best, even if they do not really work. I have seen people who, already giving sixteen hours a day to a project and blinded by fatigue, feel obliged to put in one more hour when their performance begins to drop, rather than take time to restore and put energy into the energy bank. When our ego self has extended our effort way beyond itself it has also removed us far away from the influence, nourishment and wisdom of our own mindful heart. We feel cut off from any spiritual source, prey to our fears and compelled to keep on the weary, repetitive way. We are afraid of stopping because this means facing the edge and the unknown. We fear falling off into a terrible abyss. We fear our emptiness. We fear our internal pain. Or we cannot find a logical reason for why we should feel so exhausted and begin to add shame to our build-up of inner feelings.

There are also times in all our lives where we just cannot stop. Having to work hard to support a family, to compete in a diminishing job market, to look after elderly parents or difficult teenagers, we are exhausted by constant emotional demand and there are times in all our lives when we cannot let up.

We may also become exhausted by loss and defeat, by our striving to give our all only to be met with ingratitude and more demand is an exhausting and defeating experience.

So, we carry on, even egged on by defeat, with more determination and effort, as if running from the creature following us; or, from that sense that we are just a hair's breadth away from the opening chasm behind us. And the more we carry on in the old way, compounding our exhaustion, the more desperate we feel, the harder we try and the more fixed and obsessional we may become in our thinking. We are like Sisyphus pushing the boulder up the hill; or feel as if we are trying to push the river. We have this sense of fight in us, fighting to try to gain control or 'get back to normal', but the more we try, the less we feel we achieve.

We may remain in this state for two or three years. Then it takes just one apparently small thing, like someone shouting at us in the bank, or the car going wrong or a neighbour's cat, to be the trigger to our collapse. The breakdown point is when we have overextended our effort and will-power to the point of collapse. The collapse may come in the form of an accident, heart attack, or mental breakdown. The collapse heralds our journey of return to the centre again and an opportunity to be in touch with the energy and voice of the heart. This is the time to rest and to begin to heal.

EXHAUSTION EXPERIENCED

Exhaustion can be experienced in different ways.

Body

Stiff neck and shoulders. Tension throughout limbs and in joints; hyperventilation and chest pain; small accidents; sprains, breaks, muscle spasm. Menstrual difficulties in women, loss of sexual appetite, or excess-compulsive sexual demand.

Feelings

A need to keep in control by repressing feelings. Swings of mood from feeling tearful to furious rage, feeling empty and afraid; feeling lost.

Mind

The *ideé fixe*, obsessing on getting things done.

Intuition

Largely blocked, but leaking out in swings of superstition and the need for superstitious rituals.

Recognizing our state of exhaustion honestly and naming it can be the beginning of relief. After this comes both the practical issue of how we address our exhaustion – how do we stop for long enough to let our bodies return to a healthy balance? And how do we cope with the fact of our exhaustion psychologically? While exhaustion is always created by our response to life, and sometimes we do have to live in some very tight corners and edges, learning about our responses to demand always helps us to create a more robust attitude for future demands.

CREATIVE BOUNDARIES

We need to create edges between different aspects of our lives so that our time is divided appropriately. As outside, so inside, we need to create boundaries between time for others and time for daily self-renewal. We cannot give out unless we receive in. If we are unable to be still enough or open enough to be in a position to receive, our well of giving and effort will run dry very quickly.

THE PLACATION TRAP: NEEDING TO BE NEEDED

Some of us find it hard to say no when we need to. This can lead to taking on inappropriate tasks or spending time with people we really don't like. Why do we do this and where does it come from? People who tend to exhaust themselves often have a poor sense of their real selves, who they really are. They often give out or try to please others as a way of gaining self-esteem or a sense of self. Inside, they may feel empty and hollow. Sometimes people say 'I don't feel there is anything inside me'. Work, or other people, then become the main focus and while this works well and esteem is gained, this success is dependent upon constant giving out, effort or activity. The self suffers and has no place, and the person is not in contact with the self. It may pull and tug, in dreams of running to catch a disappearing train, in the pain in our necks, in the sickening fall in stomach, but if these stirrings are banished as shameful or judged as weakness, we do not address them. It then takes something dramatic such as a collapse to bring us round to meeting ourselves. Our collapse or breakdown point takes us into darkness and meeting unconsciousness. We may remain in this place for a time and need help and support to restore our balance, to learn what it was that brought us here and where we go next.

It may be that the part of us which has been dominant in our lives has actually run out of energy because its time of dominance is up. We do not move in a linear way, we do not use the same parts of ourselves for one lifetime. Parts of us wax and wane.

'It is illusory to hope that growth is but an additive process requiring neither sacrifice nor death. The soul favours the death experience to usher in change'.[1] What is it in us that is exhausted and ready to let go? What are we hanging onto that it feels so hard to let go of? Identity? Power? Face? Skill? External goods? Beauty? Attachment to substance and control?

Many of us are unaware of the difference between the ego-adapted self and the inner self until we have a crisis. Crisis brings

---

[1]   Hillman, J., *Suicide and the Soul*, Spring Publications (1976).

these issues into focus. But we can become aware of our tendency to hurry sickness, to be colour-blind to fatigue, to try to run past our own exhaustion. The wife of a cardiac patient who had recently died said to me: 'He behaved as if he could run past death itself'.

KEEPING WELL

Keeping physically well while enduring times of hardship and exhaustion is extremely important as is developing the rituals which will keep us well. It helps to pay special attention to the following, as if you are developing your muscles for a marathon crusade.

Sleep

Make sure you have adequate and restful sleep and note how you feel when you wake. If your sleep is disturbed, you suffer early-morning waking, find it hard to go off to sleep, first try to acknowledge that all is not well and feel into what it is that is preventing you from proper rest. Images are again helpful here. Note the images that surface throughout the night and write them down. What is trying to communicate to you in the dark of night? First we need to hear, and then we need to get some rest. Find a regime that helps you rest, such as physical exercise, abdominal breathing exercises and evening relaxation and visualization. There are many herbal aids to restful sleep available in health shops such as tincture of hops, passiflora vervain. If your sleep is seriously impaired, you may be suffering a clinical depression or physical illness and it is best to take medical advice. When you have explored all these and still your sleep is suffering, then let it be and see what comes to you. After meningitis, I did not sleep for more than three-quarters of an hour for over nine months. After three months when I felt deranged by fatigue and was cross with my body and impatient with the process I lay awake in the small twilight hours and received the following communication: 'if something as major as initiation is going on, you just cannot sleep on the job'. It made sense and I surrendered to it. And, at the same time, made sure that about once every ten days I took a small dose of the lethal concoction prescribed by my GP which brought me seven blissful hours of unconsciousness.

Breathing

Watch your breathing and make sure you are not hyperventilating. Hyperventilation produces fatigue, feelings of breathlessness as if not getting enough air into the lungs. It can contribute to dizziness, tingling in hands and feet, light-headedness and chest pain. Ideally, find a good teacher to show you how to do abdominal breathing and practise this three times daily until it comes naturally. If you have been able to begin mindfulness or meditation practice, you will notice how this practice will bring your attention to the nature of your breathing.

Diet

When we are exhausted, we tend to eat on the run and grab easy food often full of salt and fat because they carry the illusion of feeding our fatigue. They don't, they only make things worse. We gain weight and feel heavier, get indigestion and feel bad. Try to bring ritual into your eating, always sit down at a table, sharing it with others, and to eat healthily and see it as a positive contribution to this time of exhaustion.

EXERCISE: LOOK WITHIN YOURSELF

1 Feel behind your own exhaustion, into your body. How does it speak? What does it say?
2 Name the part of you who has become the driver in your life. What is he/she/it like? Where does this figure come from? How did it get there? What keeps it in charge?
3 Note the difference between the driver self who is hurtling

around in circles trying to gain control, and all the aspects of yourself you are neglecting and leaving behind.

4 What do these aspects the driver leaves behind wish to say? What is the voice of that which is at risk of being flattened? How can you listen to this self and bring it more fully into your life?

5 What does the driver with its hurry sickness serve? What is your fear if this part were to step back?

6 Spend some time risking the feelings of emptiness you may be running from. Just allow them to surface and feel their rawness as much as you are able. How can you bear witness kindly to support the feelings of emptiness in order to allow something new to come in? Why can't I say 'no'? How can I learn to know how and when to say no to the illusion of demand in order to listen to the space that follows?

7 Find the well or the source of nourishment we sit at each day, even if for only five minutes, to contemplate this place and image of ourselves drinking from the great eternal wellspring of life's fresh water that will water our parched spirit. However busy, however impoverished our daily life, this image will always be there for us. It is our attitude of accepting its great bounty that we must foster, especially in the midst of our exhaustion. The water of feeling and the water of human kindness. This can let the parched begin to feel softened; the thirsty to drink and the swollen to become healed, the burnt-out regenerated and the flame of exhaustive fear quelled.

8

Loss and Fear of Loss

Falling, falling, into the dark, into the unknown dark,
unbound after swaddling.
A glimpse of love presses the limping Chinese feet
Emptied of hope
The unvisited ocean swell inside calls me
to unveil my eyes and leap into its vastness.
I fear it is too big for me
so I bargain with my sad trifles,
in the basement of the psyche,
in small mindedness:
If I do this, behave well, ask for little
will you send me a kind messenger?
I go over and over what has been, what might have been; if; if only;
I keep it small this way and the ocean swells beneath me.

E. W. McCormick, private collection (1994)

A deep sense of loss and being pulled down into it, like into death, is part of the darkness of the edge. We feel we are cut off from some central link, from some unnamed vital source within, and are at risk of spinning into the vortex or abyss. We feel loss all around us, wondering how we ever felt linked to anything or anyone of substance. Who are we and where are we going? We are not in charge.

Our body feels as if it has lost a limb. We are hollowed out as if by a blow to the solar plexus; or, in our guts there lies, like molten lead, a permanent feeling of dread and terror; our hearts are broken. We yearn for reparation, for restoration. It is as if we have been abandoned and cut loose by the mighty hand that once held us in its palm, and that now there is no hope for us, we can only fall and keep on falling, descending by both night and day into darkness. And, on the way, we meet all the other figures who have feared the fall and gone into it.

In Dante's *Inferno*, he writes 'I was so heavy and full of sleep when I first stumbled from the narrow way'. In this lost, stumbling journey through the dark wood Dante finds again consciously his innocence and sense of self. In her commentary on the *Commedia*, Jungian analyst Helen Luke writes: 'There is only one thing that can save a man in such a pass. It is to admit that he is completely lost and just how frightened he is, and to force himself to look up and away for a moment from self pity and absorption in the ego'.[1] When we begin to look deeply and remain truly present with what is happening to us, however frightening, we are developing a more robust attitude to our life and we are also nourishing the potential for a transpersonal thread. Often, the potential for this thread is our only guide throughout the darkness. Then, rather than just plunging into the darkness, blindly, we step with the small light of our awareness and reflection. This becomes like the light of a small candle to take into the darkened unknown.

UNIVERSAL LOSS

A sense of loss lingers like a trace element in all our life experiences and is a profound aspect of being human. With birth comes loss, as we leave the apparent safety of our private experience with our mother's womb where our life began. Some of us always carry an image of the paradise garden where all is green and bountiful and long to return to its bliss and safety,

---

[1]   Luke, H., *Dark Wood to White Rose: Journey and Transformation in Dante's Divine Comedy*, p. 5, Parabola Books (1989).

wanting to revisit this image in all our close relationships, whether human or divine. Our experience may be reflected in the warmth of a close relationship, but it can also include feeling suddenly excluded from the paradise garden we have come to expect or believe we need to be attached to.

There are birth experiences which leave us with images linked to the tomb or cage, with associated suffocation and entrapment. We then may well spend our lives running from any closeness that might claim us back into this dark dungeon. And if we have not been able to experience separation appropriately and the boundaries between infancy, childhood and adulthood are not safely crossed our relationships may be dominated by regressive swings back or having to rush away in panic. The liminal nature will call until reparation is made and the crossing born.

Our coming into the place of the edge may well be to do with an event that has again asked us to attend to our attitude. Until we can stand alone and make relationships from a place of individual separateness, we are unable to forge the capacity for true togetherness with another. For coming together in the true sense means always accepting difference and separateness. At the edge, we are in private relationship with ourselves, with the opportunity to forge a greater mindfulness of the threads within us.

LIFE TRANSITIONS

Other transitions in life that involve both ending and beginning such as going to school, leaving home and getting a first job, moving to university, building our first independent home and family also carry aspects of loss. We may not notice the loss because we are intent on pressing forward into the new. Any change involves loss of what went before. This is marked according to our previous experience of loss and the feelings already attached to loss. Major losses in early life through death, illness, depression, divorce, constantly moving house or country, may remain like unexplored parcels within us, waiting to be opened by the appropriate trigger. Our own stages of life and development also carry many different experiences of loss, of childhood innocence, adolescent freedom to experiment, woman or manhood during menopause, challenges to identity after job loss or change in status, during social, cultural or financial adjustment. When we are on the edge, our feeling of falling into darkness, losing what we know, particularly of ourselves, is acute.

We may have arrived at this place because of actual loss of something important to us, a job, status, money or a loved person or animal, and therefore are in a state of shock and grief for that loss.

GRIEF

Grief has its own peculiar melancholy and madness. It is physical. It makes our hearts quiver and palpitate as well as feel as heavy and cold as a stone. In *A Grief Observed*, C. S. Lewis writes: 'No one ever told me grief felt so like fear. I am not afraid, but the sensation is like being afraid. The same fluttering of the stomach the same restlessness, the yawning. I keep swallowing'.

Grief hurts. It turns our legs into jelly and makes us feel sick. It dries our mouth, confuses our brain, turns our thoughts into repetitions. We obsess about trying to turn the clock back to when things were 'normal'. Our normal is gone, so is our ease, comfort. It turns us in on ourselves, forces us to live narrowly. In the narrowness, we feel small and undone. In the narrowness, we forge spaces we had not thought possible before. We see everything through a veil of tears. We feel as if we will never be happy again.

Loss can make us feel paralyzed and sick, misunderstood and bitter, paranoid, suicidal and misunderstood. We may feel betrayed, angry, vengeful. We will feel powerless, victimized, tearful, sick to our stomach and left pining for what was, for what might have been, our hearts in agonized ache, brimming over with the weight and poignancy of our deepest sadness. C. S. Lewis writes about his conversations with Joy, with wondering where she is, wondering if she were suffering the separation also. He struggles with his god who took her away from him so soon and returns to admonish himself for his ramblings. Although feeling angry, even ashamed about 'this horrid little notebook', the notebook is the thread with which he revisits the spiral process of his grief over the first year and comes to see the process as a whole. It is both thread, and container for feelings and ramblings.

Grief brings us deeply into ourselves and in connection with everyone else who has felt grief. The entire world. While personal loss makes our vision narrower, it may also offer us the opportunity to feel more connected to whoever or whatever is god for us than ever before. The breathtaking nature of death shatters illusion. It awakens us to impermanence. It can release us to live.

Grief is a universal experience in response to loss. All of us experience it, whether our loss is conscious or unconscious. Sometimes, when we lose something or someone important to us, we are awakened to losses that have gone before which we may never have named. Loss makes us aware of our attachments and the place these attachments have in our sense of ourselves and our choices. Loss of a relationship means not only missing the person, but also having to live without that person and everything they carried for us. Grief may be for a person, a belief, a way of life, it is part of the aftermath of illness and change. It may be grief for unlived life.

LOSS OF SENSE OF SELF

Actual loss may be the trigger for an awareness of deeper inner loss. The feeling of loss experienced as being on the edge presents us with a particular deep dread connected to the constant and unfathomable fear, the fear of the loss of self.

We may be awakened by this most fearful dread. The dread of losing a self with whom we have never had a proper relationship. Our dread tells us that we must return to connect with the self within us and to not do so is to court psychological death. The self may have called to us before. We may have been touched by this in our dreams, our waking thoughts and longings, in our images and our sense that there is always something *else*, something beyond the everyday, beyond what we know. But if we have not acted upon this call and returned consciously to our inner life to forge a link with our self, the thread that links ego and self is not strengthened and the axis upon which our lifes' dance revolves is unstable, even broken. If we have not nourished the inner 'real' and given space to listen to its note or allowed it to show us the way, we feel like an empty shell. If life is lived only through the ego and persona, which alone cannot give us the bridge upon which we explore the depths and transcend the known, we remain impoverished and in fear of losing out. Our innate capacity for wisdom and compassion is not widened and developed.

Actual external loss such as the threat of our losing our own life through serious illness or accident can awaken in us a terror of dying that comes from our fear of never having truly lived.

What Alice Miller calls the 'provisional life' is the life lived only by the overadapted ego personality within its severe limitations. In a provisional life, we are still living as if it were too dangerous to be our real selves, that in claiming this self our security from the outside world would shatter, exposing us as the inferior, weak, shameful, unloveable person we fear we are. Many of us build very successful provisional lives in the outside world and shine through our external achievements. And for a while these achievements may make us feel good. They work because they help us to emerge into adult life feeling a bit safer. But if this world is built upon the sandy soil of an overadapted or survival self it will not last. Something will herald change. When we have had to cling on too tightly to our provisional life, because of a fear of returning to childhood pain, we may have surrounded ourselves with all the edifices of power, position and money. Those things we hoped would give us a sense of self and a ground of being. Then the fall can be great indeed. So, through accident, illness, loss, we return both to the original sense of loss of self experienced in childhood, and to the opportunity to refind our own innocence and from this build a greater sense of who we really are.

LOSS AS PREPARATION FOR DEATH

People who look at death all the time have a different attitude to life from those who are strangers to death. Life can become more precious because we have known the finality of death. To be able to sit in the friendship and laugher with someone who you know has experienced the severest of losses is to be in the presence of someone who has lived the extremes and walked the narrow way between. To be so much in the moment of life is a fantastic gift. To have glimpsed the fact of death, to know the brush of death's wings, to have had death take away that which was loved, and to then return into life willing to live every moment shows a robust truth and magnificence.

NAMING AND DEFINING THE IMAGE OF OUR LOSS

In accepting the reality of our sense of loss, we need to try to locate the different levels of the loss we feel and write them down as external losses and internal losses, naming them fully and all the feelings that accompany them. Sometimes we experience loss as just a black hole. Jeremy Howe, whose wife Lizzie was murdered by a student, described in a newspaper interview how he felt his grief over her loss to be like a black hole which was swallowing up his whole life. It was suggested to him that he define the black hole, as small or large, a place into which he could look or around which he could ring-fence. Once we have named our loss and the image we carry for that loss we too are able to choose how to relate to the image in our everyday. Some days we will not be able to look at it at all and other days we will rail against its death-defined boundaries. Other times we will return to it with a sense of the observer in us, or with the wisdom possible through transpersonal energy and ask for help as to the meaning of this loss in our life. And we must enter a period of grieving for that which has been lost or neglected and begin the task of mourning.

Psychology names the four tasks of mourning as follows:

1 To accept the reality of the loss.

2 To experience the pain of grief.

3 To adjust to the environment in which the loved/desired/ beloved is missing. This may apply to our hopes, aspirations, beliefs as well as to actual persons.

4 To withdraw the emotional energy and reinvest with another relationship. The opportunity, as Jung said, to begin a love affair with one's self, to explore our own reality, and to energy untouched by our response to others, for the time being.

Buddhist psychology goes a step further than western psychology as it embraces the fact of suffering and loss and the fact of impermanence. Trying to recreate what we have lost only makes us suffer more. So finding ways to be present with loss and grief is a mindful practice for accepting the nature of impermanence, that everything changes, all of the time. This is a stark image of the true nature of being alive and in practice each of us could benefit from meditating upon it every day. It can help to free us from the burden of becoming overattached to things and to people because of our fear of loss and our need of them to avoid loss, rather than the beauty of the exchange with them. This can compromise remaining truly present with another person we love and who they are, the love we feel for them and they for us, those moments we can share in being together.

EXERCISE

1 How does your experience of loss make you feel? What are the different feelings you are carrying? What is your image of what you feel? Write them down.

2 What are the resolutions you realize you are making about your life that are a reaction to your loss? For example, I will never try anything again, love again, hope again.

3 In recognizing now an awareness of loss in your life, have you grieved for this loss? If not, how can you enter this liminal phase and grieve actively for something or someone you have lost, so that you may honour this experience and soften the edges of your loss by the tears and waters of expressed grief?

4 If you feel you're falling and clinging on, how can you choose

to jump, move, swim into the next stage? What climate, geography are you in? What do you need in this place: walking boots, water wings, skis? What will help you take the step into the unknown that has called you?

5 When we begin living each and every moment, remaining present with the nature of that moment we are not looking back or rushing forward, we appreciate every single facet of our lives. Loss makes us intensely aware of the precious and precarious nature of life. How might you make a relationship with loss so that you know its savage demand but are not reduced by the bitterness of blame or self-pity, but emboldened to embrace your own gift of time?

9

Grey Melancholy and Black Depression

Grief may sublime itself, and pluck the sting
From out its breast, and muse until it seem
Etherial, starry, speculative, wise,
But then it is that Melancholy comes
Out charming grief – (as the gray morning stills
The Tempest oft) and from its fretful fire
Draws a pale light, by which we see ourselves
The present, and the future, and the past.

Bryan Proctor, 'Melancholy', in *Dramatic Scenes and
other Poems* (1857)

The great spectrum loosely called 'depression' reaches between grey melancholy and black depression. Part of the human condition is to feel 'down', sad, blue, low in spirits, melancholic in response to disappointments, loss, difficulty and to the awfulness of many world events. To be cast down is appropriate in many circumstances.

When we are in the dark and we cannot see, we have to learn to listen, or to move slowly through the dark touching and smelling things, developing our awareness of other ways of being in the world, and other functions within ourselves. In our melancholy, we have time to be with ourselves, think alone, not have to be pulled into others' needs or be in the limelight. In sadness and melancholy, we may take time to visit or be visited by images and the landscape within the unconscious sphere.

Melancholy can also be seen as a necessary time of slowing down to aid recovery and gives us opportunity for healing. For artists, writers and poets, the melancholic state is a necessary place within which to create. The half-light dims the glare of everyday demand and allows an intensity of feeling and the passion needed to survive to emerge.

Beyond the greys of melancholy are the deeper and darker demands of depression. They feel organic, heavy, they fill our every pore, they take over everything about us, body and soul. Our thoughts are slow, confused and frightening, our feelings are either numb or splintered, our body and senses feel separate from us. We are prey to odd ideas and a fragmented sense of ourselves. We may feel persecuted, paranoid, defenceless or overwhelmed by rage. Often, in a full-blown depression we are literally only in the dark. We may need to be taken care of, looked after. It is later that we see we have actually forged links within what can only come from this journey in and through darkness. In this place, we remain long enough to no longer be able to falsify the truth. When the ego cannot rise and take over, we forge unforgettable and unfathomable links with soul. And whereas we would never wish the dark experience of depression consciously onto anyone, we may come to realize, after our sentence is passed, that what we have gained is a priceless intimacy with ourselves and the nature of our despair.

In grey melancholy and black depression it is winter in the psyche. The life force feels on hold, suspended, out of reach. Our world is all one colour and muted patterns, nothing stirs, growth is completely hidden, everything feels the same day after day. It may be difficult to know when the process of grey melancholy, necessary for reparation, healing and for creation, moves into the darker shades of grey and sinister black and our state is then more accurately described as one of depression. We are less in touch with reality, feel possessed only of our internal landscape, enjoy nothing at all, where we feel ourselves to be on an irrevocable sliding slope to nothingness. At the severe end of his own long depression, William Styron writes:

I had now reached that phase of the disorder where all sense of hope had vanished. My brain had become less an organ of thought than an instrument registering, minute by minute, varying degrees of its own suffering. The mornings themselves were becoming bad now as I wandered about lethargic, following my synthetic sleep, but afternoons were still the worst, beginning at about three o'clock when I'd feel the horror, like some poisonous fogbank, roll in upon my mind, forcing me into bed. There I would lie for as long as six hours, gazing at the ceiling and waiting for that moment of evening when, mysteriously the crucifixion would ease up just enough to allow me to force down some food and then, like an automaton seek an hour or two of sleep again.[1]

When examining with our observer approach we need to consider the two polarities posed in this place of depression. The value of grey melancholy on one hand, which is necessary for our wider, deeper communications with our internal landscape, and the paralyzing catatonic results of deep, intractable black depression on the other hand. The observing midwifery approach is to watch, support and encourage, to trust the process within, even when the path upon which the traveller labours seems to open up perilously or reach a dead end. When emergency looms, it would be irresponsible and misguided hubris not to intervene, in order to offer the real meaning of the word asylum. A safe place from the hostile threatening world experienced in severe depression where torture and humiliation are omnipresent becomes the first bridge to healing and stepping out of the black chasm of depression.

William Styron, in *Darkness Visible,* writes:

I am convinced I should have been in hospital weeks before. Hospital was my salvation. The hospital offered the mild, oddly gratifying trauma of sudden stabilization − a transfer out of the too familiar surroundings of home, where all is anxiety and discord, into an orderly and benign detention where one's duty is try to get well. For me the real healers were seclusion and time.[2]

---

1   Styron, W., *Darkness Visible*, Picador (1992).
2   Styron, W., *Darkness Visible*, Picador (1992).

VINCENT VAN GOGH

Van Gogh lived on the edge all his life. He suffered a lifelong omnipresent though sometimes hidden depression, but his upbringing had taught him to value melancholy. His father told him 'sadness does no harm but makes us see things with a holier eye'. In 1876 Vincent was a preacher in England. He wrote in his sermon 'Our nature is sorrowful. By the sadness of our countenance the heart is made better'.

Vincent moved within melancholic states to the extremes of black depression, almost glorifying suffering, and marginalized himself by his social isolation and shabby dressing, not looking after himself or eating properly. The Van Gogh family had high expectations and demands, and several of Vincent's siblings had low self-esteem and emotional problems, one was schizophrenic and two, including Vincent, committed suicide. Vincent describes his image for himself as a young infant as a 'seed exposed to a frosty wind'.

In his psychological biography, Lukin writes: 'the story of Vincent van Gogh is a never ending struggle to control, modify and glorify or deny a deep rooted melancholy and loneliness. Religion and art were simply different means he employed for this purpose. He [Van Gogh] says "the work helps me avoid that melancholic staring into the abyss". He made a distinction between what he called "active melancholy" which was ideal for painting, and a paralyzing depression which leads to despair'.

'Treatments' for depression in all its mysterious guises and colours will always be hotly debated. Van Gogh's troubled inner life will be the subject of different views for many years. What if Prozac had been available? Or psychoanalysis? Perhaps primal scream or transactional analysis? Or, what if Vincent had been able to heal his early frostbitten wounds within the transcendence of a loving relationship? What would his paintings have been like? But his story serves to offer us a powerful archetype of suffering and torment as the brilliance of his paintings and that archetypal wound they convey to us speaks to generation after generation and needs no fashion or creed to be identified.

FORGING A SOUL WITHIN THE VOID

Different people experience depression and melancholy in their own personal way. The hallmarks of black depression are a sense of unrelenting pain and misery with no hope of change. The hopelessness about our situation, that it will never change, weighs heavy on our whole being. It is hard to contact any light or believe in anything good. In this place of deepest darkness, all the lights are shut down. Whatever transpersonal connection we have forged before may feel eclipsed or hard to hold onto. Often we have only a token awareness that there is indeed somewhere this light being held, for us, by others, by the collective force of transpersonal energy which is the light that ultimately redeems the suffering of the world. These are times when this is all there is, and those holding the light for us in whatever guise hold our soul in their hands. This is the most poignant time and our experience of travelling within this dark cave of depression when all else is given up may make us feel that we can no longer find any sense of God, whatever God is for us and however strong our beliefs have been previously. This can be the point of utter darkness when we feel forsaken by everything that has gone before, by those who have been with us before, and the beliefs we have held before. It is also true that in this place where we cannot find God, we come closer to God than at any other time.

This is the time when our relationship with the God within is forged in the depths of our own soul. The temptation will be to cover up any threat of entering the place of the void with ritual and false beliefs. We may search in organized religion for comfort. We may be told just to pray, or be chastised because we do not believe enough. 'Oh ye of little faith' is a note that may lead us to search for ways of naming our experience of God. We may find our own way into the energy of the God or Buddha that lives within us and is responsive to our opening into it. The fact of the existence of this transpersonal light is evident from stories of others' travels along this way. Scratched into the walls of one of the Jewish basement ghetto places in Poland are the words:

I believe in the sun even when it does not shine;
I believe in love even when it is not shown;
I believe in God even when he does not speak.

Evidence comes to me daily of individual struggles with holding onto glimpses of this light in the darkest of places. What helps people through this place is the fact of others' support and belief in them in the simple daily reminders, the cards, letters, phone calls that make *all* the difference. I was moved by hearing on a radio programme in the USA of an army debriefing colonel who had to sit in his Washington office listening to the stories his men had had to process from the Muslim massacres in Bosnia. Men tortured, their wives and daughters raped in front of them before having their throats slit. One day after telling his individual horrific tale one Muslim soldier left the army barracks and hanged himself. Each lunchtime the debriefing officer, in despair over what to do with these horrific stories, would cross the square and visit the Vermeer exhibition. An exhibition which has claimed the love of the world since this date. As he sat and gazed at the luminosity of Vermeer's work, which captures the essence of presence in its most tender and everyday form, he learned that Vermeer too lived in a time of violent civil unrest in Europe.

Our personal melancholy or depression may be entered through a variety of experiences. Loss which is unable to be mourned, anger which is unable to be fully expressed, a long time struggling with the weariness of exhaustion and depletion frequently result in what we loosely term depression. Depression seems to be an umbrella term used to describe these painful but indeterminate experiences. Many books and articles are written on depression and many approaches claim 'success'. But we must ask: what do we hope for out of our encounters with depression? Is it depression into another layer of our being, a going down meaning a deepening, an opportunity to forge a greater robustness for being in life? Depression seems so often the very essence of being human. It is part of humanity's response to an inner or outer world which is terrible that brings us into this place. Not to admit to depression, to try to medicate it away or to attempt manically to run past it, overbrighten it, would seem to diminish our capacity for depth of feeling. Statistics show that most people come out of depression, however deeply they have been thrown into it. And many people come out of depression with a greater sense of reverence for the beauty of the world as well as the darkness and misery. It seems to me that reports of depression have increased alongside the growth in demand for excellence. A balancing factor perhaps in a worldview that could become polarized. To get depressed is to get real; and it demands us to weigh the balance between what is manageable and that which becomes unmanageable.

EXERCISE

1 Where do you feel you are on the spiral between grey melancholy and black depression?
   Make a chart for yourself showing the times over the last few months when you have moved between the two. Mark on the chart what times brought you in contact with each and write down something of what was happening then, what you were thinking, doing, involved with and any images that come to you from that time. Keep this chart for the next few months and let yourself feel in touch with the language and the quality of the rhythm being shown to you.
2 Find an image for grey melancholy. Paint this image and note the language of its geography. Then find an image for your depressed feelings, from the everyday awareness of feeling depressed to the blackest place. Begin to become aware of what this image refers to and what it most needs from your understanding.

Negative, depressed thinking

Sometimes depression is compounded by negative or depressed thinking about ourselves and our situation. In this way we build what Dorothy Rowe refers to as a 'prison' for ourselves where our thinking confirms a sense of our own worthlessness. Negative thinking can be a trap in that because something has not gone well we presume that other things will not go well and we begin feeding off our gloomy thoughts presuming that our future will be coloured in this way. By recognizing the trap of negative thinking, writing down the specific negative thoughts we catch, we can begin to stand back and ask is this true? Or, is there another way I can approach this?

Unresolved loss

If we find that images of depression take us back in time to some unresolved loss from the past, then part of our journey upon the edge is to recognize and meet the pull-back to address this loss in whatever way we can. As we said at the beginning, we are all wounded beings. When the energy still in the original wound calls to us, it directs our life force into that place and we can only enter it and work within it, finding those who will accompany us on that journey to resolve what has previously been unresolvable.

Change

This too will change. When the natural time has passed and something is resolved, then the dawn in our psyche begins to awaken and the frozen winter begins to thaw. It is time to emerge from darkness and to be awakened. Some people report surprisingly strong volts of feeling beginning to come into their depression. A greater clarity, an actual sense of lightness or divine presence, a greater sense of beauty and connectedness to other people and to the things of nature. One or two people report transcendent and spiritual awakenings where a being with a divine energy shines forth or delivers a message of welcome. These experiences may be in moments only, and there is still the journey to make through the daily routine of depression and melancholy. But the moments of lightness may move us along enough to go gladly, accepting the shroud of depressed awareness, until such time as we are able to emerge fully. And many people report the emergence from the pits of depression as being like a rebirth.

10

Anger and Rage

Heart again – not fear but battered
Like a mortar shell
Blows a hole
Chest like bedsprings, punched, a dull thud,
Instant shut down
Again, again, again
Why hope?
Life ebbing away year by year
Elastic hope returns
To teenage cynicism.
Black humour, no laughs now.
Tired, tired. Wasted effort.
A wasted life.
A con worn thin
Who cares?
A few fireflies in the distance
Sporadic, cheering
But too few, too peripheral
Too ungraspable in the yawning abyss

A world of goodness I cannot reach
Too derelict to try, to think, to hope
For contact.
Too frightened to get what will keep
Me alive will kill me.

Marjorie Orr, 'Let Down' (1995)

The edge spirals and whirls like a spinning top, blurring clarity. As we are spun round, we are stunned, then angry, twisting in anger; then, lost in the process, caught in the spiralling momentum of rage, beyond ourselves, beside ourselves, out of reach.

Anger can have a useful positive form, and also a negative destructive one. Anger can be the motivating force that arouses our passion and fire, that initiates, names feelings, trumpets our boundaries, clears the air, gets things moving, tells us how much we and others care about something. Anger never inspires indifference!

In its negative form, it becomes something we fear, in ourselves and in others, so we tend to avoid it in others and bury it in ourselves. This means that a head of steam may build up inside us as it collects all our angry responses down the years that have been repressed and smiled over by us. Repressed feelings of anger can emerge far more violently than those expressed immediately and then let go of.

There are many facets of being on the edge that invite our anger; why me? Why now? Anger is a first response to unfairness, injustice, being taken unawares, lack of power, being out of control.

These feelings are more acute if we have reached a time in our life when we feel we have got it about right. We've done all the right things, taken the obvious knocks and medicines, been a good person, read the right books on personal growth, had therapy, said our prayers, enjoyed modest success and fulfilment, supported others, and the rug is pulled for the rats to start biting. Just as we think we've got it all in place, everything changes.

We may be tumbled out of a job we believed was secure or a relationship we held dear, or our sense of connection to belief or life work is seriously challenged.

The rigidity and narrow sharpness of the edge, full of unknowns and fears, can make us feel punished. It's as if we are on trial; or, we've been tried by an unknown court for an unknown crime and been found guilty. We feel as if we are serving time in punishment. We know we are angry somewhere, but our anger may feel far away, or disconnected from us because it is so hard to pinpoint the actual source of our anger. In impotent rage, we can feel as if all the world is laughing at us, has seen our folly and judged us an outcast in crime, and will make us suffer.

We feel as if we are at war, but there is no outward sign of a war on, there are no uniformed regiments to join and flags to fly in support of the effort; no obvious cause for which we can fight the enemy. The enemy is within us and we see it everywhere. We feel under constant attack and, at its extreme, is persecution and torture. The images flow only too graphically: being on the rack, strung out; held in the stocks; flogged by some sadistic jailer; flayed by the strap. We feel teased and tortured, pressing first on our anger, then our rage and then driving us into rage-driven oblivion.

When something we've held precious is taken away from us for no apparent reason, we feel naturally outraged at first. It can be hard to find expression for what we feel and to understand it.

What have I done? What is it? If only I could know, then I could put it right, make amends, get something done. But no one is saying. The world goes on around us: business as usual; can't they see that we are floundering and seething, that we are a deranged prisoner caught in a trap, our appeal pending?

This is one of those times when we are thrown into anger as an immediate response to being thwarted. But our anger has nowhere to go. We are suddenly not in charge. We are being invited to move along paths we would not consciously have chosen but they are what our life has brought us. There are two choices. Either we learn to be truly present with the depth and roots of our anger, looking deeply at all the thoughts and ideas that are arranged around it; or, we can build on our anger. This might mean taking it into ourselves and becoming self-destructive, hurting ourselves, or passive-aggressive, a martyr one minute and brute the other. Or we can lash out in blame or vindictiveness at whoever will take the hook – our parents, history, fate, railing at a harsh god. This feeds our righteous indignation and builds a fatalistic attitude of being unlucky.

BILE AND BITTERNESS

Before we can absorb the full meaning of how we might use our anger and rage, we must dance in and out of their devastating rhythm. Naming what we feel as anger or rage and bearing witness to the range of feelings surging through us is our first step. We allow a raging against the world that has let us down, a kick against the belief we feel has bottomed out, relationships that have not held. We recognize and bear the sorest place, the brittle inner fury against ourselves. That awful feeling that we went wrong somewhere, we got it wrong. We bear witness to the going over and over past events. If I had done this, done that; not done this or that. If I'd been different. If they'd been different. Round and round the same bit of the spiral.

This kicking and spitting-out process brings us in touch with sides of ourselves we have never known. Someone who fell in love for the first time at the age of 50 with a scoundrel who gave her the deepest delights and the deepest sorrow said after the second betrayal 'now I know what it feels like to want to stick a knife into someone'. Anger verging on rage is visceral, physical and urgent. It calls us to pay attention fully to its physical demand. In doing so, we make a relationship with this visceral demanding raging torrent. This means our acceptance. We do not act first, we do *not* stick a knife into someone, but honour the blade of our rage. This may mean putting our blade somewhere and into an object that can take the energy and transform it – the earth, water, clay. And to find words and put energy and passion into them, to scream and shout and yell out. Our rage and bitterness, the greenest bile all must be honoured in this grittiest, dirtiest dungeon of rage. But catharsis alone will not transform our anger. In fact, too much catharsis may water the seeds of our anger and nourish it. We may need to honour and acknowledge what anger feels like physically and then find ways to express it and be with it.

Once we really feel how devastating being possessed by anger can be we never treat it lightly or allow it to direct our action. Once we respect its power, we become awake to its quality and we learn to say: '*hello my friend, here you are again. I must sit with you and feel your storms until I understand you and know clearly how your heat needs to inform my action, my words*. And then there comes the cooling aspect of relief from the possession of anger. Perhaps of all the emotions anger is hardest to bear witness to. To not be taken over by it and not to avoid it, but to remain truly present with the fire and storm in order to understand it.

To not honour the feeling viscera of rage is to harden our anger into emotional bitterness and seek literal revenge or to let our bodies take the strain. Anger hardened down into artery and cell wreaks havoc with our homoeostasis. John Hunter, an eighteenth-century physician, wrote: 'my heart is in the hands of any rascal who chooses to annoy me'. He lived out his belief by dropping dead at a medical board meeting after an argument. Perhaps he had not found ways of being angry that were safe. 'My tongue will tell the anger of my heart, or else my heart, concealing it, will break' says Kate in Shakespeare's *The Taming of the Shrew*.

Fran's dream went like this:

> I am standing in deep piles of shit. It is other peoples' shit as well as mine. Some is old and hard and some is fresh. It is disgusting and frightening. I feel I will never get out of it. Then I look up and there is a shower in the ceiling which begins to sprinkle soft, gentle water onto me. I let the water wash me clean and watch it wash away all the piles of shit.

When we looked at this dream, she related the standing in shit to her current job. She had agreed to take on a difficult assignment to please a powerful female boss to whom she was unable to say 'no'. Her boss was herself a very angry woman, often losing her temper, shouting at others, and finding anger in all the corners of her life. Fran had admired this woman because of her energy and hard work and had been happy at first to go along with her plans. She also could see that she hoped some of her forthrightness and fiery energy would rub off on her. Fran had always been afraid of anger, feeling it to be a mark of rejection, so she sought to placate her boss's demands to fend off what felt like an attack, driving any anger she herself had deeper inside her. She became a puppet to the woman's every demand with her own qualities unvalued and undermined making her feel put down, a weakling (and like shit) if she did not give in.

The dream graphically shows the layers of shittiness in which Fran was now up to her ankles. Old shit from the past to do with old angers she had never felt free to express and the new layers from her current situation. She felt that the actual substance of the shit was her own anger she had disowned. She recognized a life of 'swallowing' her own responses, when up against powerful people and she was being forced to recognize (to stand in) the end result of this swallowing, in the waste and decay of her own repressed feelings. She had taken other people's shit as a matter of course, smiling and pleasing and not minding. The key to change shown by the dream was the looking up. It is when she looks up, away from her need to take shit from other people in order to be liked, and at another dimension, that the scene changes. Looking up can be seen as taking a step aside. In doing this, she moved to look beyond her immediate and limiting situation. At that moment, before the cleansing waters flowed, she became linked to a transpersonal dimension. She came into this by being willing to stand in, bear and look at the shittiness of her life. The ability of transpersonal energy emerging in such a place lifts us from the dark unseen into the light and joy of seeing. This movement brought the flow of water with its cleansing, healing properties which connected her to flow and rhythm. It also showed how easy it was to let go of anger once you decide to just look up!

When the Zen Buddhist monk Thich Nhat Hanh heard that six of his fellow monks had been killed in the war in Vietnam he went out into the woods for a whole day and walked with his anger. In his book *Anger: Wisdom for Cooling the Flames*, he offers us this meditation:

> Contemplating the damage from anger to self and others I breathe in.
> Seeing that anger burns and destroys happiness I breathe out.
> Seeing anger's roots in my body I breathe in,
> Seeing anger's roots in my consciousness I breathe out.[1]

---

[1] Thich Nhat Hanh, *Anger: Wisdom for Cooling the Flames*, p. 214, Riverhead Books (2001).

HOW ANGER DEVELOPS

There are many layers to anger. We may have naturally a fiery, angry temperament where we rise up like a flame in response to whatever angers us then die down quickly after the flaming, unaware of the heat arising. We may have grown up in an angry household where the angry response was the most common one, and we grow up either joining in and comfortable with anger, or recoil from it, avoiding it wherever possible for the rest of our days. Some people grow up familiar with anger as part of life, as a healthy response to some situations. It emerges and is then gone. Anger is then not feared. Some people who have never seen anger because it has been submerged by a deadly coolness are unaccustomed to angry outbursts and thus afraid. Conversely, some people grow up too used to uncontained or worked-through anger being around all the time.

Rosemary said

> I've had huge amounts of anger and I'm just getting to a point where I'm allowed to feel something else. The big problem with anger is you have to let it burn itself out, but with me if I'm not on one extreme then I'm on the other, so, if I'm not for, then I'm against and I have to be against [powerful figures] because otherwise I'd betray myself. Very dangerous being in the middle ... then I don't know where I am.

Sometimes our angry insides become projected onto others who then have to carry it for us. Governments and British Rail are often popular for this, as are public or media figures who behave in ways that invite our anger as well as confirm our reasons for keeping anger under wraps – Saddam Hussein, Slobodan Milosevic, the Al Q'eida network, George Bush; the mythological figure of the Medusa. As we fear and avoid anger, it can become very split off from us and we are not aware of carrying it.

There is a habit among modern therapists and social workers to insist that people are angry and tell them so even when the person is quite unaware and out of touch with any angry feelings. Not until something draws our anger and it enters our bodies can we know it and only then can we claim it and work with it to express the layers of it. It is no good in abstract. If, from hearing someone's life story, we think they should be angry because of the injustices that have happened to them, and evidence tells us that they are unaware of this dimension in themselves we have to accept this. Life may provoke their anger in the natural course of things and we would hope that when this happens they are then ready to manage it rather than be blown away by it.

Many of us do not dare to be angry because we have witnessed what terrible things uncontained anger can bring. And others have perpetrated upon them such terrible deeds that they are beyond anger and their sense of self is held together by not being angry but by being on hold just in order to survive.

But the place of the edge brings us into our own anger. It is terrifying and it is also a relief. Anger is like a terrifying and tremendous storm that can feel life-threatening, and can cause devastation. Some things do get swept away, but after a timely storm, which long has been brewing, the air really is cleared and the smell is sweeter than ever.

CRACKING OUR PERSONAL MIRROR

Many of us survive and mould ourselves on others' acceptance or admiration of us. This means that our sense of ourselves is conditional upon others' views and upon our keeping these views. We may live for a long time quite happily on these compromised terms although our relationship with ourselves, with others and with life itself will tend to feel impoverished and limited. But we do not know why. We may get pushed to the edge because of this sense of impoverishment or, if all our identity is caught up in this adaptation, when we lose it we feel devastated. We have been seeking others to mirror back our bright ego personality and suddenly that mirror is cracked and we are thrown back on our inner sense of impoverishment and prey to bitterness and rage. Some of the rage is with the actual event – the person who sacked us, stole our money, or the lover who rejected us. But far, far deeper and more powerful are the energies of a self who was once marginalized by not being seen at all. If we have only ever been loved for the face we show to the world that reflects our parents' or others' glory, we become like an object of their command and learn to gain this objectification in our relationships. We dress, keep fit and smart to be a beautiful reflection for others; we work hard and strive to gain admiration which will preen our peacock feathers, we strive for perfection and believe our safety and sense of self is at the end of that rainbow. We are devastated when it does not work any more. And yet this fall from grace is our very beginning of real felt life, to be truly alive and in the world with all its beauties for their own sake. To not have to try, struggle, strive.

Mary Oliver writes:

> You do not have to be good,
> You do not have to walk on your knees
> for a hundred miles through the desert, repenting.
> You only have to let the soft animal of your body
> love what it loves . . .

In Ovid's myth of Narcissus he describes the long, increasingly desperate search for an appropriate mirror for the self, and the responding 'Echo' from one's own voice. It is possible to transform the rage, envy and bitterness left at the denial of true selfhood that may be exposed after the 'fall from grace'. The pain of this loss of self, often described in psychology as the pathology of narcissism, is to a greater or lesser degree, all part of early human experience and can occur at any time. In *Narcissism and Character Transformation*, Nathan Schwartz-Salant writes: 'a psychology that recognises the archetypal power of the Self can also consider the devastating effects of envy, without seeing it simply as a too-negative concept that is consequently of little use'.[2]

We have to put the old, worn mirror away that we keep showing to others, stop looking outside for reflection, admiration and feedback to give us a sense of self-worth. We've done that and it no longer works. Now we have to give birth to our own real self, the self that will bring us answers from inside.

---

[2] Schwartz-Salant, N. *Narcissism and Character Transformation*, Inner City Books (1982).

TURNING ANGER AND RAGE AGAINST OURSELVES

Sometimes our anger is so hidden and unconscious and we are so gripped by the misery and unfairness we feel has been caused us we can only rage against others and ourselves. We cannot see any redeeming features or positive outcomes. And if we drive others away in fatigue – for even the most loyal friends are sorely challenged by our breast-beating that goes on for too long – then it's as if we have no one left but ourselves to turn our anger against. This is the time when we are most vulnerable to begin a journey of self-hate and self-destruction. We invite the suicide within us into the ascendency. We can recognize this by noting our attitude: 'why bother with this?'; 'who cares anyway?'; 'I may as well be dead'; 'no one will miss me'; 'It'll be better when I'm gone'.

We may become a victim, seeing persecutors everywhere, unable to take in goodness. This is the darkest place on the edge, the tightest corner. *Our challenge is to widen up, to speak to others of how bad we feel, to practise postponing harming ourselves.* How long can we give ourselves? Another ten minutes while we make a phone call? Another day when we make a visit to someone? And, if we can recognize how desperate we are, then perhaps we need to give ourselves up to a trusted person to take care of us for a while, until this desperate annihilating storm has passed. We will look more deeply into this place when we consider suicidal impulse in Chapter 15.

EXERCISE

Questions we might ask of ourselves in the place of anger:

1 What part of me is angry? What is it like? Find an image and then draw, paint, sculpt. Ask yourself: is this image connected to the ego that wants its own way?
2 Where does this image come from? How long has it been there? How old is the image? What are its characteristics? What does it remind me of?
3 If it is old anger, what needs to happen to it?

4 What purpose does my anger most serve, right now?

5 How can I honour the focus my anger holds for me in ways that I can usefully manage? How can I take responsibility for this anger, get used to saying *'This is my anger and no one else's'*.

6 If my anger has never been expressed, what do I need to do to express it, let go of it in myself? Write letters, write a story, dance a furious dance, punch bags, stab the earth? And after this private, contained expression, how do I then let go of the anger and restore calm to my body and mind?

7 What in me is so angry it wants to die?

8 What in me wants to be born?

MEDITATION UPON ANGER

Sit with your breath and notice:
breathing in, I know that I an angry
Breathing out I know that I am angry

Breathing in I honour my anger
Breathing out I honour my anger

Seeing anger's roots in my body I breathe in
Seeing anger's roots in my consciousness I breath out

Determined to work at the roots of anger in me I breathe in
Determined to work for the release of anger in me I breathe out

11

Vulnerability

Come into my most sacred place
Loot my abandoned dwelling
I've left myself to make myself acceptable
Coming to your house as your respectful guest
So the shell that is me is vacant and vulnerable
Most of all it is valueless
Because I have left it
I indiscriminately trade myself to make me lovable
Something so easily bartered must come cheap
And is treated so, transgressed against and violated
The issue of prostitution
It is a cruel irony that I give so much for want of love
To find myself horribly lost and without
Dimly I see the panic under which I function
The distance now grown between me and my home –
A sense of belonging
Moves towards reconciliation inspire panic and terror
Messages of compassion anger my suspicion
While my nerves screech with awakening intolerance
As the brutalisation of habitual street walking
Can no longer numb the hurt of neglect
Caught between two worlds
A looted building and a fugitive.

Belinda Ackerman, 'The Issue of Prostitution' (1994)

On the edge, we feel so exposed. So much of our usual way of being has been stripped away from us. We feel as if we know nothing any more and our vulnerability glows like the skin of the hermit crab who has outgrown its shell and needs to find another place to live. Sometimes we feel like Prometheus stranded on a rock with birds pecking at our soft viscera. We feel stuck in our vulnerable place and victim to the elements. We have lost our defences. We feel like a little child, and for the moment are a 'being' vessel without the protection of the original nursery or learned ego shell. We have to endure the pain of not knowing how to be or what to do and imagine that the ground is being prepared for growing, for something new to be born within us. Many of the initiate paths involve being rendered down, or actually broken in order to be reborn. Within the chaos of disintegration, we must hold onto the image of the gestating fledgling.

CORE WOUNDS

When our core wounds open we feel again as if we were that tiny fragile young child who was once abandoned, hurt, crushed, teased, humiliated, tortured, damaged. None of our well-learned coping strategies work for us, and we feel stripped bare. As we revisit our core wounding, we have the opportunity to use our adult-learned consciousness to bring light upon the core, and to bring those feelings and experiences which have been buried into the present time. Core wounds do not go away. What happens is that as we move about the spiral of life experience we meet our wounds differently. In revisiting core wounds we have the opportunity to ask: what needs to be healed?; what needs to be strengthened? This job cannot be done while we are swinging along in the energy of ego consciousness in full flight. We have to give up this part of us, or have it given up, so that all our concentration is upon the inner core place. Using the power of the image is helpful.

How do we experience our own wounding and what is the nature of that wound. What is our image now of our vulnerable, our most fragile self? Where do we carry it – in our feeling

151

nature, our mind, in our bodies. We cannot force, pry, cajole our way through a journey of this kind. We have to be rendered down into it in order to be within it. Our truest, most authentic answers come from this place.

These are times when we need to ask our observer self to be alongside the process, befriending and guiding us when we feel lost for words, helping us through.

Core wounds are invaluable as they keep us human, they remind us that, as humans, we are vulnerable and fragile. It is in this totally vulnerable place that we have the opportunity to be open to a place of meaning beyond suffering. We also come closer to what is transcendent for us. Our place within spaciousness allows us to be closer to transpersonal energy to feel a nearness to divine energy, and to the presence of the divine. Our experience of what we may name as god within us, our Buddha nature, our link with a transpersonal 'self' grows through this experience of confrontation with base reality and mortality. The wonder of God or Buddhahood cannot grow except through confrontation with human values.

SELF-ESTEEM AND THE NATURE OF THE WOUND

The experience that brings us onto the edge can offer us information about what aspect we are asked to strengthen in this barren place. If our core wounding involves difficulty with feeling, and leads us into a crisis in relationships, then perhaps this is what we are being asked to revisit in order to have a different relationship with ourselves and our feeling nature. Many people ask in their loneliness, why does this keep happening to me? When we examine our patterns, the way we make relationships and the terms on which we make them, we may find for example, that there is a pattern of choosing people who need us because we need to be needed. As if only by being needed do we gain worth. And, although this may work for a while, if people stop needing us, or we begin to feel taken for granted by others' dependency, we feel exposed and vulnerable again. As well as resentful. And we may never have learned to express what it is we really feel or want. So others do not actually know. When we are exposed to our fears, based on the old belief that we are unloveable unless we act, do, give in a certain way determined by others, we can question: does it need to be like this? And the next step is to begin to release ourselves from the bonds of conditional love in order to take new risks, and to check our newly discovered muscles with a new attitude. We will always be vulnerable to fears that we are not loveable unless doing what others want, but we can learn not to be restricted and conditioned by this old belief. As we do so the old beliefs will get fainter and fainter.

There is a story told by Mark Epstein in *What the Buddha Felt* of the puzzlement of His Holiness the Dalai Lama when he heard that the most frequent problem faced by western people is low self-esteem. The idea of self-loathing, self-hatred, self-dismissal was alien to him. Western psychology attempts to understand this by naming early experiences of parenting as being either too much (modern parents striving to be everything to their child thus leaving no space for a child's world) or conditional (too intrusive and invasive). Or the opposite, being too absent – leading to a feeling of aloneness and anxiety. In the middle there is the 'good enough' parent who allows a child to be alone with him or herself in an atmosphere of confidence and love.

When there has been too much or too little emphasis upon developing the unique selfhood of each individual person, we become much too dependent upon other's opinion and much too thin skinned to others' responses. When we have a fragile ego, we are always looking to others to reflect back a favourable self. When we have a too rigid ego, we can get so turned into ourselves that we let no one near to us and remain unreflected by others. A regular, disciplined way of life, of work, practice and looking outward to others and the world, sharing in community needs, helps us to loosen our dependency on others for mirroring and approval. This may emerge naturally in our lives through the work we do or community we serve. Or, we may seek an enforced period of containment where we are able to develop the robustness we need so that a human vulnerability is happily present within us.

BEING A VICTIM

Falling prey to victim thinking is one of the pitfalls of the vulnerability of the edge. Every time we say 'he left me' or 'she made me', or 'I was all right until he/she ... ' we are pushing blame onto another and casting in stone our victim mentality. When we abdicate responsibility, it binds us to others in a way that perpetuates our sense of helplessness. It may be painful to say 'how can I look at these things that keep happening to me?' or 'what is it in me that keeps attracting these things?', and it may take time before we can come to this place, but, in taking this step, we reclaim a feeling of control. Our self-pity soon passes as we begin our investigation, which can take us beyond our own individual patterns to look at the family we came from, the world family and into the realm of archetypal reality.

PUER AETERNUS

Many men and women carry the theme and energy of the *puer aeternus* in their relationships. They may have a string of short-lived, intense relationships because they are in love with being in love and are afraid of the ground of commitment which makes them feel their wings are being clipped. If they cannot fly, they die. This energy can cause deep heartache all around, for those who are left with a broken heart and those who carry the wound of fear of suffocation and who can appear heartless. Pushed to the edge, the dance becomes a slow waltz between redeeming the pain of feeling grounded and suffocated, caught in another's web, and denied one's spirit, and honouring the magic and exhilaration of the flight – those colourful butterfly wings that can so initiate and charm. The two-way dance is for those who carry this archetypal energy and those who are attracted to its enchantment.

BODY AND MIND EDGES

Our body may bring us to the edge and become the messenger

of new consciousness. The edge may be inviting us to have a new relationship with our sensation function, with how we use our bodies and the matter and substance around us. It may be a better balancing act that the psyche has in mind. For example, if our core wounding involves the confusion of our feeling and sensation functions it is the separation of each that allows us to realign. Many of us submerge feeling into our bodies because there is nowhere else for it to go, and we let the body take the strain. We don't do this consciously, we simply swallow our feelings or build body armour around them. It is not coincidental that expressions such as hard-hearted, lionhearted, open-hearted refer to the way we present our emotions through our physical presence. Another misappropriation of feeling is to go up into our heads and take on the 'thinker' pose. Many people can identify with the idea of coping by 'rising above it' and living it in their heads, inviting the thinking function to think its way through our feelings for us. The expression of feeling or unmanageable states via the vehicle of the body, called somatization, is seen by analyst Joyce MacDougal as an alternative to something nearer to the chaos of madness.

ILLNESS AND ACCIDENT

If we have lived too much, or for long enough, in our heads, in the airiness of the thinking function, our edge may come when we are grounded because of illness or accident. And it's not that we have done anything wrong or bad, it's just that psyche may be inviting us to readdress the wound to our instinctual, sexual or physical body because the time has come for this. This is not to say that all accident and illness is because of a need for balance. Accidents and terrible illness happen for reasons we may never know. But how we approach the very present drama of illness and accident makes a difference. For a moment we are the victim again, prey to the fear and helpless rage that this creates, and we may have to go through this first. Then, when we are ready, we can move on to be the investigator, the explorer, finding out everything about the intimacy with our physical body nature that our experience has brought us into. When we are ill, our body is right in front of us, calling to us in its suffering. We are invited into the deepest possible relationship and respect for the way it speaks and moves, together with our thoughts and images. We have an opportunity to use this particular edge as a magnificent bridge between inner and outer worlds and watch the interweaving between the two.

There are many mysterious illnesses today, given names such as ME, postviral fatigue syndrome, chronic fatigue syndrome, post-traumatic stress disorders, and allergies to substances, that go on for a very long time. They ground us, bringing us into what can feel like a twilight world of vulnerability, also bringing us into the opportunity of a new relationship with body, instinct and nature. The strange, often undiagnosed illnesses often present with similar symptoms to depression. The search for diagnosis and treatment can move from the biological edge of medicine into the complex and mixed edges of the psychiatric and neurological professional world. As stories of ME sufferers show, this is always a painful journey. Is it the body, or is it the mind? Am I believed? Is my pain 'true' in as much as we tend to view what is true as needing to show physical evidence.

Anybody suffering from malaise needs to be taken seriously and a plan drawn up for care. It is often only after an exhausting journey through many doctors and potential 'cures', when anger, anxiety and exhaustion have risen, that we move into a pattern of acceptance and begin to accept basic care. In suffering from physical complaints, we have the opportunity to experience the best contribution from modern medicine. But the healing process cannot begin to take place until our relationship with our physical suffering has been accepted with unconditional friendliness and, ultimately, with love. This is not the same as resignation or saintly collapse. I see it as a process of active dialogue with our physical structure whose cells have either temporarily or permanently changed. This then becomes a part of oneself that we are in communication with as it struggles with functioning poorly, remains stubborn, feels sad and worn out, or is in active 'disease process'.

In *A Leg To Stand On*, the famous neurologist Oliver Sachs writes with exquisite clarity about his experiences following a severe accident to the musculature and ligaments of his leg. He 'lost' his leg in terms of both his physical location of it and the internal image he carried of it. Deeply disturbed by this breakdown of sensation and feeling, and after his leg had assumed an eerier character he writes:

> In this limbo, when I journeyed to despair and back – a journey of the soul – I could not turn to science. Faced with a reality, which reason could not solve I turned to art and religion for comfort. It was these, and only these, that I could call through the night.

There are many current studies from psychoneuroimmunology and from the alternative approaches to medicine that have researched the relationship between personality, energy flow, consciousness shifts, life changes and the effects on the body. Eastern approaches to the body work with the whole person, and with the central images of the nervous system and the immune system as being central to well-being. When we address the core, it seems, by whatever metaphor, inner or outer, we move into a different relationship with ourselves as a whole, and perhaps true healing begins at this interface or bridge.

DEPENDENCY

When we have to take time off work, from commitment in order to look after our most vulnerable needs or actually be looked after and receive the care of others, we are at our most vulnerable. It may be the first time we have had to receive from others in such a way and we may be terrified of being dependent. Many core fears arise with the threat or actuality of dependency. If we have fought hard for control and to maintain control it will be hard for us to be a patient, and have to *be* patient! And, to be, like a small child, without power or trappings of any kind. We will inevitably go through a whole spiral of difficult feelings related to this experience. At the same time, a part of us will be hugely relieved. To have to carry on working and giving to others, meeting deadlines when you are feeling ill and fragile is a terrible conflict. Many of us fight on to the desperate end we so fear 'giving in' to vulnerability. We fear being picked off like jungle animals by stronger animals who covet our place. But to use the time, and often we need a great deal of time in order to come into and meet this place properly and be quite rendered down, can be of such immensely valuable proportions we can emerge more grateful for the experience than we could ever have imagined. Only by accepting the reality of our being dependent can we become truly independent.

Time, and within that time, the dance between one's attitude to ego and to self, seem the crucial ingredients. When we are grounded in this way, we are slowed right down. Often we cannot move much or think clearly. Reason and physical action are suspended.

We are in the world of feelings and intuition, we can only listen to the voices inside and wait for the threads to come together.

WHO HAS THE BODY?

Sometimes it is helpful to imagine which part of us has the body at any one time. When we are feeling particularly fragile, or in pain, or feeling confused, to ask: who are you in there? And to allow an image for this personality, its colour, shape, size, quality. Paint or draw the image, name it, speak with it, ask it about itself. Get to know it as it keeps appearing in your struggle. Befriend it and allow it to have a life within you. Some people discover caged birds, prisoners in a cell, fugitives, bonsai trees, dwarfs and Gypsies who have been without position or words living within us only able to use the body as communication. The following poem came out of my own experience with meningitis.

My body knows something before I do.
In its tightness, its hurt
the way it shuts down
it is saying something that I cannot.
The inner artist paints the wound on body's blank canvas.
tunnel headache, black and blind
ears thundering bells of doom
nerves stretched on the rack of life
the purple red of a bursting heart.

Body becomes the last refuge for
what has lost the right to speak
the rejected and the unborn
a prison dustbin.

Early on in life, who gives us words for feelings?
'I'm scared' 'I'm cross' 'I'm lost'
'I think my little sister will take my place'
'I want Uncle Arthur to die.'
Body and feelings are civilized early
tailored to fit.
Bound with expectations as a prisoner is bound with prison bars.
Don't feel just get on with it.
Don't stop until you achieve something
Don't weep pull yourself together
You'll get over it
You're no different from a thousand others.
Body becomes prison and prison guard
over imprisoned feelings
swallowing hardening diverting
and the soul quietly starves in the darkness.

Until the day of liberation
until the body refuses to be the mediator
without a union card
and the colours of the prison dustbin cover the canvas.
Feelings now run through body's bars
a language that will not lie
or lie down
smoulder, stab, ache, burn, cut, steam, boil, creep, pull, snag, fester
to unfold a story. My story, that *will* be told.

ASYLUM

Sometimes we feel so vulnerable we have to take time out to protect ourselves.

Sometimes we need to be free of the daily demand and grind in order to let scar tissue form over our vulnerable wounds, and for our open state to be taken care of.

It is always difficult to find places of real asylum, where we are allowed just to be vulnerable for a while and not be expected to do much. Psychiatric hospitals seem to take on this role for most people as convalescent homes tend to be for those recovering from an identified physical difficulty. It would be ideal to have places where we could go to recover from the burnout of life, to spend unstructured time and be basically cared for at minimal expense or fuss, but sadly these places are rare. The expensive health farm or spa seems available only to the few and even then their programmes can be active and overpositive. But, once we have realized what it is we need, asylum can be offered through friends and family, by the familiar, by a caring community, until such time as we find our feet again.

POSITIVE ASPECTS OF VULNERABILITY

1 It is an opportunity for acknowledging, knowing and healing an aspect of core pain to make way for its transformation.
2 True humility can be gained only through acceptance of vulnerability. Spiritual practice is always rooted in a position of humility.
3 We have the opportunity to receive care and kindness from others and they to give it to us. If this is a new experience it is profound. We never forget our humanity after this.
4 After being rendered down we may be reborn.
5 We have an opportunity to come closer to the divine energy within us.

PITFALLS AND DANGERS

1 In our vulnerability, we are open both to positive support and energy coming in and to false prophets and those who seek to 'save' us. We need our guides and trusted others to hold a positive thread that is right for us, while we find our way.
2 Too much exposure can cause weariness and temptation to give up.
3 Too raw and we bleed too heavily; we need the 'wise midwife' who knows when to call in appropriate help.
4 The desire to blot out pain with medication is strong. Some medication support such as mild tranquillizers are a help only

in moderation and only for crisis times.

5 Holding onto only a literal translation of our pain limits our experience and can result in our searching endlessly for the professional who will offer us a 'cure'. It can become a wild-goose chase, only adding to our burden (see Part Three).

12

Aloneness And Alienation

The smallest fragment can open a door inside the heart.
Even in the midst of bleakness,
lonely, and alone
When time is not a friend
and the grey dawn only blackens
There can be
this
bliss

Elizabeth McCormich, from 'The Pearl of Great Price' (1994).
unpublished

Here we reach a point of no return, when we are most extended. When we feel so alone in our bleakness. When we can feel as if we are alone in all the world. The last person left.

We make this journey on the edge alone. While we may well be guided by the footsteps and whispers of others who have trodden this way, no one can do it for us. We are ultimately alone within the privacy of our personality and the music of our soul. And it is precisely this journey alone that forges the inner dialogue we need to have with this deeper, emergent relationship within ourselves that frees us from the clutter and chatter of our preoccupied minds.

Many people say to me: 'Oh, why do I have to do everything on my own?', meaning 'who will hold my hand, tell me what to do?'

We can hide and escape and imagine that things are better in a crowd. We can be seduced by activity or by losing ourselves in relationships. But aloneness is vital here because we really do need to clear the space to hear what is really going on.

THE INTIMACY OF ALONENESS

When we shift from seeing aloneness as connected to another's attitude toward us – abandonment, rejection, indifference – we move into a space where we can view an intimacy with ourselves. Within this space of real intimacy, we learn how to nurture and guard our intimate space so that it becomes the inner treasure from which all things are nurtured and grow, from which stems the true spiritual life. This personal intimate space is the space into which others come by invitation only. It is also the space within which we begin our intimacy with spiritual practice, with a sense of divine presence and with God.

If we are constantly pulled to respond to another person's agenda, another's voice or demand, we can become drained of energy and feel mindless and empty, and our loneliness accentuated. If all our energy is taken up with having to try constantly to separate ourselves from the chatter of the crowd there is less and less space for the new conversations or realizations in which we are being invited to participate. Our emerging self will not be heard by us. And we are the only ones who must hear. And, if we do not, then no one else will.

Many people cannot bear the burden of aloneness. It puts them too immediately in touch with their core pain, the pain they have covered up by coping strategies. Our western society today has developed formidable structures for shutting out silence perhaps in the mistaken idea that noise helps us to feel less alone. And, whereas people who are lonely gain great comfort from talk shows and phone-ins, especially in the small dark hours, the persistent demand to be social and have a jolly time and the noise of television, radio and newspaper media can prevent us from hearing the music inside us.

One of the hallmarks of the therapeutic encounter is that it gives people permission to think quietly about themselves and to develop an intimacy with the inner life. A sense of trust that there is more inside than ever dreamed of, that we all have within us the resources we need to love, cherish and grow happy and wise in moments is one of the great gifts that can be offered by psychotherapy.

Being free to be alone does get more difficult as life itself becomes fuller and busier with causes, campaigns, opinions, tasks – our world is full of clutter and objects. But there are also trees and gardens, oceans, rivers, woods and fields by which we might rest and from which great beauty is offered to us. We are not encouraged to be alone and the term 'loner' has today received painful and dangerous connotations. We are encouraged to be social beings, in relationships with others, and this is often judged as the hallmark of success in life, to have had happy and consistent relationships. Yet our relationship with ourselves is the very basis from which all other relationships grow. If we are comfortable with being alone and can become resourceful in this place, we make relationships of a freer basis than if we need others to fill our emptiness. True solitude offers contemplation from which we may become refreshed and grow wise.

LOVE

Our capacity for love and intimacy grows early on with our first experience of love and the nature of that love. Being loved just for oneself is the greatest gift one person can bestow on another. But many people forge their capacity to love despite never having been shown love. This is for me one of the wonders of the world. And, in my experience, it is never too late to learn to give love and, later, for it is more difficult, to receive love. By just deciding to, we can choose to be more loving. *It is never too late to have a happy childhood.* The more we practise love, the more love we have to offer and are offered in return and the more love there is to go round. All human beings long for love and thrive on its quality. When it is truly born from an authentic place it is 'agenda free'. It is not sentimental or misguided soft love but the most powerful redeeming connection humans ever make. The experience of real love toward others has the energetic capacity to change the world.

THE PAIN OF ALIENATION

When aloneness is most severe in its negative form it can feel like a state of alienation. We feel separate from others, from our social group, from any group, from the world. We feel separate from anything of meaning, alienated from within ourselves, strangers to ourselves, cast off, cut off, an alien on the planet. The *Man Who Fell to Earth* goes looking for ways to get home to where he came from. In *ET*, the extra-terrestrial nearly died because he was uprooted from where he belonged. Many of us feel like ET and we want to 'go home'.

EXERCISE

1 What is 'going home' for us as mortals? Where is home? How do we imagine it for ourselves?
2 Where do we need to really belong and who is to be our family? Within the body of mankind, who are our soul brothers and sisters, mothers and fathers, relatives? Who are our kindred spirits who have made their way via similar routes to ourselves, within whom we find succour and warmth in times of dire need, who offer us a guiding hand, a smile, a kindness that brings our weary limbs? And, in our place of alienation, we are extremely aware of who is with us along the way. Who sees us, like the woman at the well who offered Jesus water when he was on his way to the Cross, abandoned and forsaken, alienated from his life's effort? Who dares touch us like Damien of Molokai, when we feel like a leper and are abandoned to the elements?
3 Who comes searching for us when we are lost, like Virgil came to Dante in his dark wood? Who might be our avenging angel? Who notices our alienation in the midst of the crowd

and gives us the smile of welcome, the soul smile on the figures in Michelangeo's *Pietà*? Who, or what, when we look back upon dark woods or passages, has been there for us all the time?

COMMITMENT TO ONESELF AS PART OF THE JOURNEY ON THE EDGE

1 To accept aloneness for this part of your journey in life and choose solitude.
2 To become aware of the voice that moves you from chosen solitude into alienation. Note images from this place and check what they mean.
3 We need solitude within which to listen and hear.
4 We need solitude in which to practise listening and hearing.
5 We need solitude within which all that has taken place may be received in an atmosphere of maitri (i.e., unconditional friendliness to oneself).

13

Meeting the Trickster

Who was it slipped in here last night
and swapped by heart for an octopus?
I felt nothing, but in the morning
there it was tentacles unfurling
to grasp anything good or brave,
its eyes glinting, reserving the squirt
of black, for anyone coming too close.

Mark Dunn
New poems 2000–2001
Private collection

The energy of the trickster tends to bring a demonic note into
our lives and is very present when we are on the edge. It is as if
we are having to contemplate two worlds, the 'real' world of
everyday reality that we have known and the hidden underworld
of peculiar irrational episodes and delight. In earlier cultures,
tricksters were known as the delight makers because they
contained the pure instinctual energy which was present before
consciousness reached the level where it could observe and
objectify what it saw. Tricksters have a dual nature, half-animal,
half-divine, and are able to change themselves into other forms,
play magic pranks. They used to appear in carnival culture or as
the court jester, the fool, in folklore as Tom Thumb, Stupid
Hans. They appear stupid because of their state of pre-
consciousness but they also possess tremendous powers of

healing and transformation. If trickster energy is continually repressed or taken literally, it can take on a more extreme demonic nature that we would call devil. In the Golden Age, figures carrying this energy were seen as the forerunner of the 'saviour'. They were god, man and animal all at once, subhuman and superhuman and unconscious.

It is through this level of deep unconsciousness that trickster energy communicates to us. Tricksters can turn themselves into anything and make things move about. Trickster energy is behind many of the things that go wrong for which we have no rational explanation. This energy may be present in the outside – the fairies that come in the night and steal the milk; the dwarfs who dance on the table leaving their boot marks, crop cycles, UFO sightings, hoaxes, and it may be behind the slips of the tongue, pranks – doing things for the hell of it and the dangerous liaisons that we plunge into because of this powerful energy. This energy is like its name, tricky, and incredibly exciting, compelling, and also dangerous and demonic, even leading us towards 'hell'. Once again it is our relationship with the energy that makes the difference as to its potential destructive aspect.

Trickster figures may be obvious, such as the magician or sorcerer or those figures in our dreams who are half-man, half-beast, like the Minotaur, who offer us the combination of human and animal energy. Something that combines the human rational world, and the deeply primitive instinctual world of beasts but who is also magical and can turn itself about. We don't understand it and we may feel repelled, but we are drawn into it. It gets under our skin. We fall easily into its spell, especially if we have been in the thrall of being overconscious, too much in ego consciousness for too long, too much subject to the delusion of control. The alchemical figure Mercurius and the mythological god Hermes come into play when we take ourselves too seriously, or are puffed up, engaging in illusion or seduced by the overliteral, or when we have not attended to something as deeply as we should have. About to give a paper at a grand conference one of the papers goes missing. A date with someone we want to impress for egoistic reasons and we ladder a stocking or forget to sew on a button.

Tricksters show us up, lay us bare, render us ridiculous for the purpose of naming our pride or omnipotence, our cheating and our laziness.

In everyday life, and much more hidden, are the ordinary people we meet who carry the trickster energy. Those people who prick balloons, who say the unsayable, who seem immoral. Those who charm and seduce us. Those into whose arms we would fling ourselves in rapture in order to be transported to another, 'better', illusionary world. It is the trickster voice who says 'it doesn't matter' when we feel we should obey the rules and leads us off elsewhere to play truant; who says 'just one more drink' when we know we have had enough. When to court more is to invite the addict in us to take over. The trickster has no sense of time or morality and is not interested in relating. Trickster energy is behind that compulsion for: 'Just one more bite of the cherry, just one more and I will have had enough'. And, on an unconscious level, it is the trickster who is behind all kinds of scrapes, awkward situations, faux pas, mistakes, grossness that we find ourselves in, not knowing how we got there.

Trickster energy invites us into a dangerous love affair – with the bottle, with drugs, with sex, money, gambling, with power. Trickster energy will tease us into the apparent charms of these tasty morsels and carry us far on their ocean wave and we will have a wonderful time, for a while.

As humans we have to meet the trickster energy and recognize it for what it is and forge a relationship with what is right for us. We must find a way in our human beingness to recognize and then resist the lewder temptations of the trickster before it runs away with us and we are lost. We return, saddened perhaps, but wiser and having had a good prank, to our quest as human. We will have had an adventure and it will be worthwhile – but not if we linger too long. He/she will play with us until we learn to separate what the trickster energy brings us in the way of initiation and heralding the new and what is merely gross and repetitive. For the trickster is primitive and the intent is to awaken us only, and then be gone. Events or people dominated by trickster energy will not change or grow, however much our longing, wanting, pleading, protesting, however much our illusion whispers 'this will last forever'. But we can let the trickster energy change our relationship with our creative powers, with our ability to let go and with our primitive and instinctual energy.

AWAKENING

Trickster energy awakens in us something that has been dormant or repressed or unlived. It plunges us into areas we would never choose. It pulls us into the opposite. It tears off any masks we might have been wearing. The fall from grace of high-profile people; the puncturing of the pompous; the challenging of the oversecure, overliteral, overconfident. And some people seem to carry more trickster energy than others. They live out a trickster life and bring these forces into the collective. They are often the least or the most popular, the scapegoat, the person prepared to receive and carry the shadow. In Christian imagery it is Judas who carries trickster energy which takes over and allows one of the most meaningful stories to be revealed to us for two thousand years.

Tricksters are dangerous, lethal, exploitative, unrelated, and if their energy is repressed it can be murderous on the scale of Antichrist figures such as Adolf Hitler. This is why earlier cultures always had the carnival figures, the official jesters and fools who drew out and were prepared to carry our mockery, our instinctual and primitive connections for the half-human half-animal. They, in their accepted role, could make these energies conscious and keep them in the realm of play and merriment. The crazy shows of exhibitionists could keep omnipotent power in its place. Our recent *Rocky Horror* show was unexpectedly popular perhaps for just these reasons.

If we can truly carry this edge, within ourselves, within our culture, we come nearer to the potential the trickster carries for initiation into a wider, wiser self and to allowing their role in bringing transformation.

It is when we are up against trickster energy that we forge our human capacity to be separate, with a truly definitive and discerning consciousness and that we begin to come nearest to divine. Tricksters remind us we need to see things with fresh eyes.

In *Daimonic Reality*, Patrick Harpur writes:

Hermes Mercurius does not unmask. He needs no satisfaction from the look on our faces. He forces us to unmask ourselves in the face of his emissaries – enigmatic marks on cornfields, big-eyed aliens who abduct us into spacecraft, 'frustrators' who dictate gibberish through automatic writing, entities whose revelations are delusions and whose delusions, if we persist in them, can lead to revelation. He manipulates us, knows our every thought – knows us better than we know ourselves. He is secretive, ruthless, impersonal and inhuman. Like a psychopath. Like a god. He is less the Devil than Lucifer, who deceives both in order to destroy and in order to bring light. If we do not know ourselves – that is, know, discern, heed our daimons and demons – we are easy meat.[1]

---

1. Harpur, P., *Daimonic Reality: A Field Guide to the Otherworld*, p. 172, Viking Arkana (1994).

14

Waiting

I said to my soul, be still, and wait without hope
For hope would be hope for the wrong thing; wait without
love
For love would be love of the wrong thing; there is yet faith
But the faith and the love and the hope are all in the waiting.

T. S. Eliot, from 'East Coker', Part III *Collected Poems 1909–62* (1963)

When we have been living on the edge for a long time we may feel as if we will be waiting for something to change for ever.

It is the fact of our waiting that bring us into ourselves most deeply. The other properties of the edge all describe action – how we might relate to, think about, respond to, the geography and climate of the particular place. But waiting is overall, it is the common ingredient throughout this journey. It is the one extraordinary factor which in itself, by itself is the container for the forging process. Like cooking and alchemy, we place the ingredients which we have chosen, sorted, handled, and thus related to, into a place where time and certain temperatures do the rest. As we are learning now with all research experiments, the relationship of the researcher to his or her research is the hidden ingredient that affects outcome. As Ken Wilbur writes, the thumbprints of the map-maker are always on the map. Our own experience of waiting is the process of forging our own change within ourselves. And, like the process of gestation in preparation for birth, it takes the time it takes. Too quick and we get abortion, too early and we get a premature, sickly struggling infant, too late and we are overboiled, overcooked.

Changes that are connected to our psychological foundations, to our world of learned emotional response, to our spiritual growth, do not come. There is no 'quick-fix' for the edge. We cannot paraglide off it or parachute down. We may be tempted and there are many quick-fix solutions on offer in our lives today. But the deep changes that require time to understand and practise, need a long and deep process of commitment. Our task is not to push the river, but to let it show us the nature of its flow at this current time, to go at the pace required and let it and us find its own level. This leads to a complete and utter acceptance of life's process when we know most truly that we cannot push the river. There may be small changes and adjustments going on all the time and we are best able to witness these changes when our journey moves us away from the edge enough for us to see.

There is a difference between active waiting and passive collapse and resigned giving up. Active waiting involves us in a relationship with ourselves and our everyday. It means removing any expectations or demands of the time, it means truly living in the moment. This sounds easy but it is often very difficult. We must resist our desire for instant gratification. Nothing on the edge is sorted out in an instant.

A PLACE TO WAIT WITHIN

Part of the great challenge of the edge is that the place is so narrow and frequently dark that often all we can do is wait it out. With the image for the edge that we found at the beginning, we might find another image for the place we might wait out our time, or voyage throughout the edge. It may be imagining a safe nest, building a straw fence around us, a tent or rondavel and put ourselves there imaginatively several times each day. Every day we go back to this place where we just wait. If there is water on our edge we may find the image of a small boat, canoe, log.

Within each image for our safe space within which to journey, we may furnish it with utensils, mandalas, special linings.

FEMININE PRINCIPLE

Waiting invites us to have a new relationship with the dark, with the yin or feminine principle, with the unknown. It is only when we have to wait that we begin to see things we would not normally look at. Waiting under a tree, we see the movements of the leaves, the patterns of the bark, the fruits borne by the tree that we have taken for granted. Animals, insects, scurrying about, who need the tree for their livelihoods, all become known to us. The beady-eyed grey squirrel carrying an acorn or peeling back a beechnut, the ants about a fallen leaf, the green woodpecker with his red hat and piercing call. Waiting at an underground station we see the vast array of human beings of varying body shape and dress, all in their own private worlds with their own private story making a journey to somewhere.

We will have to go through the initial chaotic period when waiting just feels like mindless nothing and we want to scream and yell and rush into something new or fill our time by busyness, any busyness. Then our time may be filled with the grey melancholy of depression, the loneliness of being alone, of not being able to communicate.

Waiting in our aloneness we begin to hear the rhythm of our own heartbeat, the flow of our own blood, the pattern of our thoughts, the whisper of the unbidden new and the unthought known. We begin to sense that something lives in us that is not of our own doing. That there really is something in and beyond our previous awareness that transcends our everyday and if it is in the process of being born to us its passage is as vital and unstoppable as any other natural birth. Our acceptance, our welcome even when we have not asked to be pregnant means that we meet the new and unexpected with our innocence and truth. This moment is captured with great reverence in several of the great paintings of the annunciation of Mary, where she sits alone waiting, in contemplation, usually doing some simple task, and she looks up and with a look of rapture on her face receives the Holy Spirit.

ACUTE AWARENESS

The edge demands our most acute awareness. We pay attention to every detail that befalls us. The limitation of ego control helps us in this process as we can only go one foot in front of the other, or just record what is happening to us on the most minute level. This means paying attention to our dreams, our thoughts, our body sensations, our feelings, to people who contact us, what we see in the outside world, the happenings within our immediate world. In this way, we forge a new relationship with our unconscious world, we allow pathways to develop that help us communicate to and from this place. It is easy to fall into avoiding the acute awareness in waiting. By filling the gap, we experience in just being, by doing, by actions of any sort. Before any action, we need to be asking what does this serve?

EXERCISE

1 Practise using your image for waiting and the vessel that is to be your container, its feel, quality, its usefulness to you.
2 Practise active waiting by keeping a journal to write down dreams, thoughts, feelings, anything of note that touches you; sayings, quotations, books, questions you find circulating around you.
3 Be mindful of filling your waiting time with too much action whether it is making phone calls, food, alcohol, inappropriate medication, people. If you feel the urge to do this, pay attention to the aspect of the waiting that feels most unbearable. Know it and be in it so that you know it, and if you cannot bear it, know that your busyness is in response to what you find unbearable. This knowledge means that you take up whatever busyness you need in a conscious way rather than in a passive, avoidant way. And forgive yourself!
4 Know that the time of waiting in the form you find most excruciating will pass. That, given the opportunity of gestation and creative outcome, there is always a passage from terrible waiting and through the threshold into the next phase, the dawn or birth of something real that emerges only after the waiting has served its time.

Part Three

DANGERS OF THE EDGE

15

False Gods

In each of the aspects of the edge, we have looked at positives and negatives. We have seen that the journey on the edge will always hold the potential for danger. This dangerous aspect can attract or repel. Falling off the edge or being sucked into the vortex is always a possibility. It is part of being alive and a fear that all humans carry.

This section looks specifically at the main dangers that can occur when energy is diverted from being present and mindful of each aspect. This occurs when we think and act literally and with tunnel vision, without allowing the dance between what is the realm of ego and what is the language of the self trying to emerge. When we do not allow what is happening to be held in the wise cloth of the sentient heart and hear the beat of that heart we are at risk of falling into extremes, into one of the opposites that our edge is trying to hold. If we confuse waiting and not knowing with boredom, for example, we may rush headlong into any activity just to relieve ourselves of this feeling. Because the journey on the edge is daunting, we may fall at the first hurdle and decide to give up, living on automatic or in denial of an inner life that calls us. We may fall at any hurdle at any time and our falling may result in disablement or in resurrection or in both. It seems as if we become at our most vulnerable when the journey of the edge stays over one place for too long and our endurance becomes sorely tested. We want a shortcut or a quick-fix solution. As we have seen so far, there are no quick-fix solutions to this path which has many tests of the ego self-axis along the way. But our longing for change may assert itself in our preoccupation with solutions and the seduction that these solutions carry.

The solutions to a way out of our predicament tend to come in the form of false gods whom we believe will bale us out and take our burden from us; or in courting what we believe will be the relief of the end through death by suicide.

FALSE GODS AND PROPHETS, AND ADDICTIONS

Many people and ideas can present as false gods, goddesses and prophets inside us. The voice of the false god or prophet declares with utmost authority: 'this will save you'; 'I've got just what you need' or 'come with me and be my love'. The offering of the false god may appear in the form of alcohol, drugs, sex, love, money, power for its own sake, new-age cultism or guru religion. The common denominator of the false gods is the powerful seduction and promise to get high and get off the fragility of the edge, to rest one's weary head on the breast or pillow of this wonderful other and be transported, as if by magic, into a never-never land where we do not have to grow up and everything bad is someone else's fault. We want the responsibility for being human and the acute loneliness this often reveals removed from us. We want someone else to tell us what to do, dictate our daily grind and ritual, to relieve the weight of the momentous journey of soul forging.

The immediate gain is often a clue as to the falseness of the god we feel we've found. We may feel so high and away, so transported beyond that which we ever imagined possible, and that, at last, this is *it*, we have found *God*. We may look back and despise where we've come from, we may reject all that has gone before, trying to discard that old struggling self as a pathetic creature who is only fit for the trash. But our 'solution' tends not to lead us into wider fields but into the narrow and desperate path of addiction where all energy goes to serve the addiction god itself. The understanding we need in this place is profound, to acknowledge the extent of our fear and terror and our longing for solution. The downside is the *crash*. When gods are false, their promise is hollow and only too quickly we are thrown back on our dependency and addiction and all the pitfalls they bring. Worst of all is the realization that our edges are still there. Whatever the promise of the false gods to relieve us of suffering or indecision, we return to face these inner issues when the path we ventured upon turns into a blind alley. And added to the burden of the edge, we have now the chemical burden of addiction, whether it is the adrenalin rush of simulated worship offered in cults, in the taste of power, or the nicotine, cocaine or crack or alcohol rush.

Following the false gods may take us on a wide detour, and it may be necessary in some way to bring us to a vital point. In her book *Witness to the Fire*, Linda Schierse Leonard writes:

> The turning point for my addiction was at the bottom of an unfathomable abyss – in a detox ward. There I faced my death, and I also clearly heard the call to life. After years of trying to stop myself drinking I felt helpless and humiliated. At that moment, on my knees in prayer, I admitted I was powerless.[1]

She writes movingly about the miracle of being with others also brought to their knees by addiction who make a pledge to commit themselves to return to life.

> I learned that this required daily commitment, a vow to life each day, and that the ultimate issue was not merely to stop the physical act of drinking but to face the very meaning of my life – not conditionally as I had done before, but with my very blood.[2]

The promise of the false gods may feel like nectar to the thirsty but the delivery is short-lived and its promise hollow. Addiction brings us to other edges. But it yet may be the place we have to come to in order to begin again.

---

[1] Leonard, L. S., *Witness to the Fire: Creativity and the Veil of Addiction*, p. viii, Shambala (1990).

[2] Leonard, L. S., *Witness to the Fire: Creativity and the Veil of Addiction*, p. viii, Shambala (1990).

DESPERATE DECISIONS

All of us can look back in our lives and see decisions taken out of desperation and in ignorance of any alternative. We may live to feel sad, even regret decisions we made – in partnerships, jobs, travel, in health, that have ramifications for the rest of our lives. There is no such thing as 'perfection'. We all have to live with these threads of desperation and try not to think of them as mistakes, but as something we chose which was based upon the limitation of our awareness then. But we do not need to do the same things twice from the same place of desperation. Once we are able to reflect, and have become conscious of our ways, our path, our tendencies, we do have wider choices, even if our only alternative to a hasty decision is just more waiting. What seems important to watch out for is that we do not allow the extremes of the feelings at the edge to push us into further desperate decisions simply because we want relief, or because we have not yet practised endurance for long enough. The question we might ask ourselves is: what is behind my sense of urgency over making this quick decision?

Consider the plight of a woman whose youngest child has just started school. She returns to work but work has changed and her attachment to it has changed. She feels scared and is unsure what to do. She could go to college to retrain; she looks listlessly through the brochures, but nothing grabs her. She has never wanted a 'career' and isn't interested in voluntary work. Staying on at the shop – work she is used to – is comfortable but not much fun. She is listless and bored. She starts hanging round the school playground with other waiting mothers, some of whom have prams and pushchairs. She begins looking in at the prams. She may actively decide to become pregnant again, or she may 'forget' to use contraception which results in a pregnancy. Her decision is made for her and her next five years are taken care of. This may turn out to be a wonderful addition to the family, never regretted, but the chances are that the listlessness and boredom will return at some point, perhaps around the time the children are about to leave home. The time of attending to these feelings will just have been postponed. If it is a happy and welcome postponement then it is of no concern. But feelings that are left to fester get harder to address and often come to a head in another form.

This same process can occur when we make desperate decisions out of a refusal to be fully conscious and present as to our state of mind and our reasons for action. We can see this mirrored in people who drift into marriage to get away from home or other unsatisfactory situations; who accept a job in another country to avoid making a decision about emotional commitment; who take a huge pay rise rather than stand up for one's viewpoint. To be bought off and rendered impotent can be a desperate decision we repent at leisure.

DRUGS AND OPERATIONS

Sometimes a way to get off the edge, if it is manifest through our bodies, is to undergo a plan of tests and investigations. I have written elsewhere[3] about the way in which psychic pain can be carried via the body and express itself in physical symptoms and pain. When this is looked at only literally and drugs offered or operations performed the source of the pain is not located but simply transferred to another part of the body or another time. Examples of this can be seen in the spinal fusions and hysterectomies that are performed to relieve the symptoms which in fact persist afterwards. If, before any physical investigation, we were able to spend time with our bodies and minds asking for an image, for questions as to the nature of their deep feelings, we might have a lot of surprises! The operations may well need to go ahead, but on a very different basis than if we just enter into these serious situations automatically and with a closed mind, making it a desperate decision. We know, for example, that many presenting symptoms such as heavy bleeding, for which hysterectomies are performed; chest pain, for which invasive tests are performed and sometimes bypass grafts offered; and knee, joint, back problems are created by the catabolic response to exhaustion when the body is so hyper-

---

[3] McCormick, E. W., *Surviving Breakdown*, Vermillion (1997).

aroused its catecholemine levels cause endocrine and adrenalin secretions in excess. To be invited off this particular edge and to look at one's relation to life, would give us a freer choice. Many cosmetic surgeries could also come into this category. It is time-consuming to go through these procedures, and many people live out their edge in the waiting rooms of doctors and hospitals. Sometimes this may be all that we can do and we need to accept that this is so and this may be our only hope of a kind and touching hand.

In medicine, we are being stretched into control issues. Should we fund transplants so that everyone may have the benefit of spare-part surgery? Wear out one heart, get another. Use a kidney, get another. The ethical dilemmas have never been so strong. So we swap one edge for another. If our desire for control has led us to develop machines that will take over life for us, those machines now, as well as perhaps giving us more life, are posing depth questions about how we live and on what terms we live.

But if we can be informed, and aware, we need to look at this process and take charge of where it could take us. Harder to move about the edge with too many medications and operation scars.

FALLING ASLEEP AND SHUTTING DOWN

We all shut down inside when things get too much. It is a natural protection of the psyche that consciousness will be eclipsed when what is going on becomes unbearable and we have no learned mechanisms with which to deal with it. This has been well documented by recent studies of children who were abused by a trusted adult when young, whose memory of the event remains hidden, often submerged within their bodies presenting as physical symptoms; or emerging in nightmares, in phobia and chronic anxiety. It may be that for some of our time on the edge we just have to shut down, to protect ourselves, to give ourselves a break. There is a difference between the conscious decision to shut down for a while and immerse oneself in a completely different activity away from the vigilant demands of the daily edge, and avoidance of the pain of the edge.

Shutting down mindfully would be travelling to a new place; reading a novel; working at a garden; cooking; digging out a pond; embroidery. The shutdown is conscious displacement of energy by diversion into another mode of being. It is always surprising what comes out of it. Shutdown of the negative kind that would constitute a wrong turning or a pitfall of the edge is if we decide to give up any idea of a spiritual quest and sell ourselves to its opposite. We opt for literalization. Falling asleep means being lured by the spells offered by the false gods. Being transported away like Sleeping Beauty so that we remain unconscious waiting the kiss of the prince. Too long in a Sleeping-Beauty trance and we are vulnerable to any false god who dresses up as a prince. Too long flying like Peter Pan, avoiding contact with the ground, renders the same effect. We are waiting, within our provisional life, for someone or something to take us out of it, hoping for magic. The edge then is the provisional life itself. The longer it goes on, the more likely we are to slide into bitterness or rage, to feel disappointed in the world that has failed us and the more desperate may be our attachments to those others in whom we invest our hope.

Falling asleep may appear in the form of an avoidance trap, which takes us on a circular route back into itself again. It is available to both conscious and unconscious aspects of ourselves. We may *need* to fall asleep at times when the reality of what is happening has become unbearable and it is our only protection. But we can keep a check on using avoidance as a habitual way of deferring responsibility or management of the pain of change. We only put off the moment of change, and this may be forced upon us by means we are even less able to tolerate than those we fear.

THE VOICE AND CONVERSATION OF SUICIDAL INTENT

This voice says 'Death is the only answer. Give up now. You've taken more than you can bear. Nothing is worth it, and anyway, it doesn't matter. No one will notice. Your death won't make any difference'. The fantasy is that death is the solution to the problems of current life. The unknown is preferable to the known. Thoughts of death as a way out begin to arise in our waking moments and our night dreams may well be filled with masks of death, blind alleys, skulls and crossbones, coffins, corpses, dying animals and children. Sometimes our longing for death means that we neglect ourselves and our surroundings. The more we focus on the thoughts of death, the more our energy supports the logic of our idea. Suddenly we find that we are thinking clearly about death and about how to bring it about, and there may be some relief that we have found a solution. The more our ideas remain unspoken inner convictions, the more these ideas become inflamed into the illusion that death is the only answer. Many people who commit suicide successfully have only alluded to it in cryptic terms – 'I'd be better off out of the way'; 'there's not much for me to hang around for', or have begun to tidy up their affairs, reduce their life's content. And in an average social situation these comments would be heard uneasily and the person reassured, perhaps comforted, but the suicide inside will forge ahead without challenge. Only reality testing – telling someone what we are thinking, that we are thinking of killing ourselves – will bring the matter to a wider perspective where we gather *all* the facts into the round.

We have said throughout this journey on the edge that we take a scientific approach, where all issues at stake are placed in evidence so that both our ego personality and our wise self have the opportunity to comment. Choosing our own death is a very serious matter. It has been the choice of many from the ill-fated lovers Romeo and Juliet, to Ernest Hemingway, Virginia Woolf, Sylvia Plath, Arthur Koestler, Bruno Bettleheim, all deeply thinking and feeling people whom we assume gave the matter a great deal of thought. But no one has returned from a successful suicide to tell us if indeed it brought the relief from pain it courted. And for millions of Buddhists, a suicidal act increases the karmic burden of the soul; for millions of Catholics it is a mortal sin. The result for both is to live with the burden of limbo, never knowing your place.

When suicide becomes a seductive answer to the psychological pain of living, our own suffering has taken centre stage and it's as if no one else exists. There are many delusions – that we are worthless and have become invisible to others because of our plight; that others must be made to suffer as we have and only in this way will we get even; that we cannot live unless we are perfect, and once fallen, we can never arise; that our sense of loss is so acute we cannot tolerate the burden of feeling for a minute longer. The pain is that we are at these times unable to connect with a person or way of significance that gives our being meaning and place in the world, which lights up our way. The illusion is that killing oneself will take away the pain and our own suicide will not make any difference to those about us.

WHAT IS IT THAT BECOMES DANGEROUS?

All of us at times think about our own death and for many the idea of death is seductive and a release from the difficulty of living a conscious life. One of the huge philosophical questions is why more people do not commit suicide, and what this tells us about the living. The most dangerous time for this question is when it is taken up literally by the logical ego and in isolation from other systems or people. Too long listening only to the voice of the part of us that wants to die means that this voice becomes insistent, obsessional and insists on being secretive. The secret is part of the seduction: no one knows what I have up my sleeve and when they do I will be gone and will have triumphed. This is the hideous cut of the suicide thrust, because suicide always leaves a trail of unfinished business and misery for those who are left behind, unresolved feelings, guilt, skeletons in the closet to haunt those who come after.

LISTENING FOR THE NOTE OF THE SUICIDE WITHIN

What is this part and what is its character?

What does it want, what would it say if it could? How can we give this part listening space and time so that we can make a proper assessment of whether suicide is appropriate for us?

Suicide is not a soul decision but one of ego personality. What is it the ego cannot stand that it wants to take everyone with it?

Naming the unbearable psychological pain and being true witness to the suffering gives us a powerful ammunition with which to enter this dialogue dance. Our conversation may carry on throughout the edge and, through conversations of this kind, we come closer to knowing our true will and basis for survival than at any other time. Only dialoguing will help these issues come clear.

SUICIDAL THINKING CAN BECOME THE THRESHOLD

Realizing how far we are on the edge of life and death is frightening. It may frighten us into rethinking life. Although there is the cocoon time, when one feels isolated and alone, the world of tunnel vision which Al Alvarez describes as 'the closed world of the suicidal being lived by forces I could not control. Feeling inaccessible, remote, out of communication. Impervious to anything outside the closed world of self destruction'.[4] Once this tunnel vision is broken, usually by speaking of one's intent or offering the image of this closed world to another, or by something spontaneous that emerges on this edge between life and death, then something new begins to happen. Even if this is just time, it is time with a difference. Time in which something else may be appraised. In his book *Darkness Visible*, William Styron writes movingly about being in this very place, when his thinking about ending his life had solidified and he had made preparation, even to the point of burying his diaries of feeling torment among plastic bags in the dustbin outside, knowing the refuse collectors would call early the next morning. He sat alone in the living room in the early hours of the morning bundled up against the chill, having torn up his efforts to write a suicide note and forced himself to watch the tape of a movie. At one point in the film the characters move down the hallway of a music conservatory, beyond the walls of which, from unseen musicians,

---

4   Alvarez, A., *The Savage God: A Study of Suicide*, Penguin Books (1974).

comes the soaring contralto from Brahms' *Alto Rhapsody*. He writes:

> This sound, like all pleasure, I had been numbly unresponsive to for months, pierced my heart like a dagger, and in a flood of swift recollection I thought of all the joys the house had known: the children who had rushed through its rooms, the festivals, the love and work ... I realized all this was more than I could ever abandon.[5]

The next day he was admitted to hospital.

Later on he describes linking the contralto voice to that of his mother who died when he was only aged 9, and to the unmanageable loss he had carried unconsciously for years. This theme of unbearable loss is expressed in his many books, especially *Sophie's Choice*. The herald to his awakening from the brink of suicide was an unseen singing voice within a movie going on in the next room. A voice calling him into life from the very edges of suicide, a voice which offered him a thread into his own deepest feeling with which he was able to choose to return to life.

---

[5]   Styron, W. *Darkness Visible*, Picador (1992).

Part Four

STEPPING STONES AND SAFE PLACES
FOR THE EDGE

16

Stepping Stones and Safe Places

So round about me shone a living light
Which left me wrapped in such a dazzling veil
That nothing else was visible to me.

'Always the love which makes this heaven restful
Receives all to itself with a like welcome,
To hold the candle ready for thee flame.'

No sooner did I take in these few words
Than inwardly I understood that I
Was rising high above my human powers.

And I was so inflamed with the new vision
That – however luminous the light –
My eyes could have withstood the sight of it.

And I saw a light flowing like a river
Glowing with ambher waves between two banks
Brilliantly painted by spellbounding spring.

'Paradisio Canto xxx'

HONOUR YOUR IMAGES

Stick with the vessel or container you have chosen in your
imagination to take you through the journey of the edge. Allow
any images that have emerged for you during this mapping of
the edge to be amplified by your life's experience and by the time
that follows. Draw, paint, sculpt, dance, make poetry and keep a
journal that honours the individual language of the place you are

in. These recordings are the Ariadne thread that journeys with you during your time in this place. However banal or painful they may appear to you at the time, however depressed and painful the recordings may appear, however little you judge you have to offer to any method of record, trust in the method itself and time will be your reward. I am still astonished at what my personal journals show to me from the times I recorded as a reluctant weary traveller. And time after time, people share with me their own experience of these matters. When we read the details and smell the atmosphere through the recordings of where we have been we marvel at just what we can come through, as well as our method of making record. We marvel at the process that somehow carries on despite what is happening on the outside.

LOVE THE EARTH

Begin to get used to the earth's rhythms and seasons and trust in these; that everything has its own season and that your time on the edge will have its peaks and troughs and deepest, darkest places, and that spring will arrive when the time is ready.

It will not be at your will, but at the gestation of the time your individual journey takes that will show you the small green shoots of new life. When you begin to smell the turning of the earth within your own life, you will know that you are ready to emerge into the spring dawn and that your ground will be wider with a harvest to come.

NEVER UNDERESTIMATE HOW MUCH WE CAN LEARN AND GO ON LEARNING

Psychology, perhaps because of the influence of psychoanalysis and its emphasis on past developmental thinking, has tended to underestimate just how much humans go on learning. Many of the cognitive therapies that are being widely used throughout the British Health Service are based upon challenging the hold of beliefs within us that we have learned in early life and which no longer serve us. When we can identify the negative beliefs that underpin our negative thinking and revise their emphasis, we can lessen the hold of negative or depressed thinking upon our way of life. This means that we can unlearn the unhelpful things we have learned which limit our life experience, and learn new ways of approaching both our inner and outer lives. And it is never too late. Janet, in her mid-seventies, found that she could begin to express herself affectionately for the first time in her life, having repressed her feelings for fear of their being misinterpreted. As she experimented, first with the children of her close neighbours, then with her cousin, she found that she could open up to her own warmth and that others welcomed it. I have found working with older-age groups, and supervising other professionals who specialize in this work some of the most moving and enlightening changes, changes that emerge just when the person is about to give up on themselves, or be relegated to a rigid drug-controlled regime.

Just because things have been in a certain way for us, does not mean that we must be there forever. Once people decide to change and to tackle the aspects they have identified are getting in the way of their hopes, loves and joys, this force of intention can move mountains. We may learn subtle and kinder ways to be with ourselves as a whole, not judging or limiting by an inner voice that says 'this is not good enough'. We may learn through the practice of self-awareness and self-respect an honesty with how things are that is able to celebrate both negative and positive. We may learn to develop an actual spiritual practice, through prayer, through meditation, through whatever regular process exercises our spiritual needs.

ACTIVE WAITING

Learn to become an acute listener to everything that happens all around you. Pick up the signs that you know herald something of interest. Because of your journey on the edge you have a unique opportunity to really tune in to the minutiae of your everyday functioning because your life by definition is narrowed down and you are likely to be much alone with your inner world.

You can get to know your dreams, fantasies, thoughts, images, longings, your body messages as well as the parts of life and people you find yourself drawn towards. You can get to know your own patterns and traits. You can become used to listening to the subtle messages of the day such as: this is a day for thinking and sorting out; this is a day for being with people; this is a day for being alone; this is a day for recording and listening to music; this is a day for searching out sacred texts and finding what has been written on the themes that are emerging for my own understanding. *If you attune your ears to the finest of sounds, you will hear all that you need to hear.*

In *Peace is Every Step*, Thich Nhat Hanh writes:

> Are you massaging our Mother Earth every time your foot touches her? Are you planting seeds of joy and peace? If we maintain aware-ness of our breathing and continue to practice smiling, even in difficult situations, many people, animals, and plants will benefit from our way of doing things.

'From the Retreat Monastery at Plum Village, France'

DISCRIMINATION

Choose carefully all that you put before you. Everything that you read, watch, hear, smell, touch. Become sensitive to the vibrations that surround you. *Everything* affects us, and there is growing evidence that we are affected on subtle energy levels by atmosphere, aura, others' vibrations, chemicals, sounds, things in the air, the presence of past and current bodies. Elaine told me of being visited in hospital after her collapse.

> I felt so vulnerable, as if I had no skin. Other people seemed to come straight at me, straight in. The nurses were one thing, they were neutral, they had their official job. When my parents came and I saw their hurt and anger behind the forced smile I heard again that childhood cry 'Elaine! not you again, what are you bothering us with this time'. In that moment I saw how I'd had to protect myself from their worry and fear, and their anger when I kept getting ill. I could see that they didn't know how to cope. And I saw, all at the same time that I must learn to protect myself in different ways from the old ones of shutting myself off or getting ill. I

196

closed my eyes after they had gone and imagined a thin blue silk cloak that went from covering my feet up to a hooded peak over my head. My skinless body at last had a veil, which did not shut anything out. I have stayed with this image and it still has enormous value for me today.

Vera wrote in her journal after receiving her first massage therapy following a long disabling black depression.

I can sense that there are some healing hands coming my way. Through the massage I have located them physically. I know that these hands have been around somewhere throughout the last four years, in the doctors I've seen, the other patients I've met and in odd moments when I stopped to talk to someone in passing. Suddenly these fleeting images are becoming visceral. When I need to I can allow them.

FIND A WITNESS

A true witness is someone who will be there throughout your journey in the most appropriate way, who has the skills of the midwife, who knows when to trust in the process and let it take its course and when to call in other helpers. One of my workshop participants, herself a midwife, said to me 'a midwife knows when to call in the experts – *only* when bleeding occurs'. If you are going to bleed as part of your edge journey, and we have seen that the edge can be sharp, choose a skilled midwife who knows their craft. Get some help in the choosing if you are in doubt and trust your own feeling. Choose someone who will let you be and who will watch for you in times of danger, who will know how to name this danger and discuss it with you, always giving you the choice of the next step but also knowing when they must act for you in appropriate ways.

FIND OTHERS WHO HAVE BEEN THERE BEFORE YOU

Choose from the ancient mythologies and stories from current literature and film, from modern heroic journeys and initiations and find a story, theme or sound which speaks to you and take it with you. Speak to the characters of those heroes and heroines, find all you can about them, let them stand as examples at the same time as honouring your own individual quest. And the people with whom you resonate may change as you change and your emphasis shifts. Allow for this, and for new characters to come into your awareness. Let them tell you about themselves.

THE STILL, SMALL VOICE

Be silent often enough and court solitude so that you may hear your true self. None of us needs to emulate others or copy more than is appropriate for new learning. Always be ready to listen and honour with your listening, the whisper or call of your own still, small voice inside. It may be small and tentative at first. It may have language that you don't like or judge as soft, silly, clichéd. Listen with maitri and allow this voice to be nourished and grow.

FEED YOUR SOUL

Find what for you is soul food. The language of the soul through music, poetry, beauty, dance, the written word or simply rhythms that honour the basic life of the soul. Read the texts which serve you in this way and return to them daily, perhaps writing them out to encourage you in the way of their beauty. Practise every day the values of a soul commitment.

WATERING THE SEEDS OF HAPPINESS

As we learn to soften the ground around us so we find more space and seeds that have been hidden have a chance of life. There are always more seeds than we think, more than everyday consciousness allows. When we water the seeds of happiness we water those moments, experiences, exchanges that fill us with joy, make us smile. Even in the darkest wood we can find a green shoot; even in the blackest day there is a hand of human kindness. It just takes one small step to accept it and water it. It does not diminish or take away the reality of our pain or loss, but it gives us another place within which we may rest a wounded heart. If we water only the seeds of our unhappiness – our anger, despair, craving – we become unhappy. And we run the risk of becoming wound-fixated victims instead of free beings who choose happiness.

WHO TO LISTEN TO

There are many people who offer advice and profound words today, many who would be guru. Be careful. Listen to what is being said and the tone it carries. Too fervent, too controlling, too demanding and you need to stand back and ask questions. Differentiate between passion which is needed as a source for life, and the fervency that comes with being *too* intent in an ungrounded, lopsided way that tries to force its point. Take note of the example of those whose words you may admire set by their own personal daily living. Someone who preaches peace and loving but who is warring arrogantly with their neighbours or manipulating outcomes is showing us a polarized picture, the Janus face. People who live by their own standards and ethics and principles down to small minutiae of how they are in shops and bus queues and who give generously to those who come their way are true bounty. They live by what they say and their lives are living evidence of their belief and standards. Take a wide view and take many views.

The words of Gothama Buddha are a helpful guide:

Do not believe in anything simply because you have heard it.

Do not believe in traditions just because they have been handed down for many generations.

Do not believe in anything because it is spoken and rumoured by many.

Do not believe in anything because it is written in our religious books.

Do not believe in anything merely on the authority of teachers and elders.

But after observation and analysis when you find that anything agrees with reason and is conducive to the good and benefit of one and all accept it and live up to it.

Before enlightenment, we chop wood. After enlightenment, we chop wood. Everything has changed inside, and yet nothing has changed. There are still chores to be done, people to attend to, letters to answer and tasks to be planned. But we come to them in a very different way. Life does not get easier, nor does it get nicer, more problem free, but our attitude to our engagement with our own mortal life has changed dramatically. We come through something and we emerge as ourselves, able to listen to our own wise self inside, not needing to be a guru or evangelist, but we speak from our own hearts as and when we find things and as we see things. We may see the world with fresh eyes, with a regained innocence and sense of wonder, delight and joy, and with our ability to receive the awe-inspiring aspects of creation, fresh and marvellous. And, because we have survived the darkest, rockiest, storm-tossed ride, we owe a debt to the mysteries of the dark.

In the same way that Persephone ate pomegranate-seeds in the underworld, and which meant she must return there for a portion of every winter, so we must make a promise to let the darkness speak to us as and when it needs and to remain in awe at the revelation of the dark's own mysteries.

Life is found at the edge and out of our struggle with the edge more life is born. There is great life to be had in our struggle between the limitations of ego and the spaces we may step into beyond. When we have been touched by a powerful numinous experience it is instantly recognizable. It may be this transcendent experience that gives us a ready place to stand alongside suffering or a simple change in attitude to suffering so that life is never the same again. The great and mighty mystery of life waits for all of us to stumble into it. We are awakened by these experiences into a more powerful connection with what for us is divine, like a rich nectar it can feed our soul all our days, whatever, wherever we have to be.

We may plan less and fret much less, we may be able to ride the huge storms knowing that they too will pass, and that it is not a question of getting through and onto the next stage, of planning when things are going to be over so that we can enjoy ourselves, it is our sacred relationship with the here and now of life that is our finest achievement.

Further Reading

This section lists books which have been mentioned in the text of the book, as well as other works which I have consulted, and which may contribute to supportive reading.

Abram, David, *The Spell of the Sensuous: Perception and Language in a More than Human World*, Pantheon Books, New York, 1996.

Alvarez, Al, *The Savage God: A Study of Suicide*, Penguin Books, Harmondsworth, 1974.

Campbell, Joseph, *The Hero with a Thousand Faces*, Bollingen, London. 1968.

— *An Open Life*, Larson, London, 1988.

Chödrön, Pema, *When Things Fall Apart: Heart Advice for Difficult Times*, Shambhala, London, 1997.

Cooper, J. C., *An Illustrated Encyclopedia of Traditional Symbols*, Thames & Hudson, London, 1982.

Dallet, Janet O., *Saturday's Child*, Inner City Books, Toronto, 1991.

Dante, *The Divine Comedy*, translated by Dorothy Sayers, Penguin, London, 1955.

Edinger, Edward, *Ego and Archetype*, Penguin, Baltimore, 1973.

— *Anatomy of the Psyche: Alchemical Symbolism in Psychotherapy*, Open Court, London, 1985.

Egum, Anne, *The Frieze of Life; A Biographical Note on Edvard Munch*, National Gallery Publications, London, 1993.

Estes, Clarissa Pinkola, *Women Who Run with the Wolves*, Ballantine Books, New York, 1992.

Fontana, David, *The Lotus in the City: How to Combine Spiritual Practice with Everyday Life*, Element, Shaftesbury, 1995.

Fontana, David, and Ingrid Slack, in *The Psychologist*, June 1996.

Grof, Stan and Christina, *The Stormy Search for the Self*, Thorsons, London, 1990.

Harpur, Patrick, *Daimonic Reality: A Field Guide to the Otherworld*, Viking Arkana, London, 1994.

Hillman, James, *Suicide and the Soul*, Spring Publications, Zurich, 1964.

— *Anima*, Spring Publications, Dallas, Texas, 1985.

— (ed), *Puer Papers*, Spring Publications, Zurich, 1986.

Hillman, James, and Michael Meade, *The Rag and Bone Shop of the Heart: Poems for Men*, Harper Perennial, New York, 1992.

Hobson, Robert F., *Forms of Feeling: The Heart of Psychotherapy*, Routledge, London, 1985.

Jung, C. G., *Commentary on the Kundalini Yoga*, Spring Publications, Zurich, 1932.

— *On the Psychology of the Trickster Figure: Collected Works, Vol 9, Part I*, Routlege, London, 1959.

Kornfield, Jack, *A Path with Heart*, Bantam, New York, 1993.

Kushner, Harold S., *When Bad Things Happen to Good People*, Pan, London, 1981.

Leonard, Linda Schierse, *Witness to the Fire: Creativity and the Veil of Addiction*, Shambala, New York, 1990.

Lerner, Harriet Goldbor, *The Dance of Anger*, Harper & Row, New York, 1985.

Lewis, C. S., *A Grief Observed*, Faber, London, 1960.

Lubin, Albert J., *Stranger on the Earth: A Psychological Biography of Vincent Van Gogh*. Holt, Reinhart & Winston, New York, 1972.

Luke, Helen, *Dark Wood to White Rose: Journey and Transformation in Dante's Divine Comedy*. Parabola Books, New York, 1989.

McCormick, Elizabeth Wilde, *Surviving Breakdown*, Vermillion, London, 1997.

MacDougal, Joyce, *Theatres of the Mind*, Free Association Books, London, 1986.

Miller, Alice, *For Your Own Good*, Virago, London, 1987.

Moore, Thomas, *Care of the Soul*, HarperCollins, London, 1992.

— *Dark Eros*, Spring Publications, New York, 1994.

Options Institute and Fellowship, 'Inward Bound', workshop programme at the Options Institute and Fellowship, Sheffield, Mass.

Perry, John Weir, *The Self in Psychotic Process*, Spring Publications, Dallas, TX, 1953.

Rumi, *The Essential Rumi*, translated by Coleman Barks with John Moyne, Harper, San Francisco, 1995.

Sachs, Oliver, *A Leg to Stand On*, Picador, London, 1984.

Scheper-Hughes, Nancy, and Anne M. Lowell, 'Psychiatry Inside Out: Selected Writings of Franco Basaglia', in Roy Porter (ed), *The Faber*

Book of Madness, Faber, London, 1991.

Schwartz-Salant, Nathan, *Narcissism and Character Transposition*, Inner City Books, Toronto, 1982.

Shorr, Harriet, *The Artist's Eye: A Perpetual Way of Painting*, Watson-Guptill Publications, New York, 1940.

Simpson, Joe, *Touching the Void*, Pan, 1996.

Sogal Rinpoche, *The Tibetan Book of Living and Dying*, Rider, London, 1992.

The Spiral Path: Essays and Interviews on Women's Spirituality, Yes International, St Paul, Minnesota, 1988.

Storr, Anthony, *Solitude*, Flamingo, London, 1989.

Styron, William, *Darkness Visible*, Picador, London, 1992.

Tart, Charles T., *Living the Mindful Life*, Shambhala, London, 1994.

Thich Nhat Hanh, *The Miracle of Mindfulness*, Rider, London, 1987

— *Peace Is Every Step*, Rider, London, 1991.

— *Anger, Wisdom for Cooling the Flames*, Riverhead Books, New York, 2001.

Tolle, Eckhart, *The Power of Now*, Hodder and Stoughton, Great Britain, 2001.

Von Franz, Marie Louise, *Puer Aeternus*, Sigo Press, Santa Monica, 1981.

Walsh, Roger, and Frances Vaughan (eds), *Paths Beyond Ego*, Jeremy Tarcher, Santa Monica, 1993.

Wilde, Kate, 'Comparisons with hunter-gatherer societies of the American continent – environmental ethic and the shamanic role', BA dissertation, 1990.

Wilhelm, Richard (trs), *I Ching: The Book of Changes*, Routlege, London, 1951.

Young, Dudley, *Origins of the Sacred: The Ecstasies of Love and War*, Abacus, London, 1991.